But you, O mountains of Israel, will
produce branches and fruit for My people
Israel, for they will soon come home.

I am concerned for you and will look on you
with favor; you will be plowed and sown, and
I will multiply the number of people upon
you, even the whole house of Israel.

The towns will be inhabited and the ruins rebuilt.
I will increase the number of men and animals upon
you, and they will be fruitful and become numerous.

I will settle people on you as in the past and
will make you prosper more than before.

Then you will know that I am the Lord. I will cause
people, My people Israel, to walk upon you.

They will possess you, and you will be their inheritance;
you will never again deprive them of their children.

*(Ezekiel 36:8-12)*

# The Face of Samaria

## The History and Life of Jews
## in the Heartland of Israel

by

**Frank Mecklenburg**

Mazo Publishers

# The Face Of Samaria

ISBN 978-1-936778-54-6

Contact the Author
Frank Mecklenburg
Zion Pathways
PO Box 1941
Prineville, OR 97754 USA
Phone: (541) 447-5723
Email: frankmecklenburgzp@gmail.com

Published by
Mazo Publishers
PO Box 10474
Jacksonville, FL 32247 USA
Phone: (815) 301-3559

Website: www.mazopublishers.com
Email: mazopublishers@gmail.com

Book Production
Prestige Prepress
prestige.prepress@gmail.com

*To all the Jewish Settlers in Judea and Samaria
who are preparing the Land for the Messiah.*

# Acknowledgments

I want to thank David Ha'ivri of the Shomron Liaison Office for his support for this book, and for arranging through his office the interviews I conducted for it.

I also want to acknowledge the help I received from Adina Lissak, Office Administrator of the Shomron Liaison Office, in translating Hebrew into English.

I also want to thank all those leaders in Samaria who offered me time from their busy schedules for the interviews that provided much of the content for this book.

I also want to give credit to my son, Ted Mecklenburg, for allowing me the use of his photos taken in Samaria.

I want to give credit and thanks to the Yesha Council for their creation of maps of Judea and Samaria and granting permission to use some of these in this book.

I also want to acknowledge the continuous encouragement of my wife, Charlotte, as I worked on this book.

# Contents

# Definitions

*Green Line:* Pre-1967 Israel border that was never established as an official border.

*Jewish origins:*

    *Ashkenazi Jew:* A member of one of the two great divisions of Jews comprising the eastern European Yiddish-speaking Jews.

    *Sephardic Jew:* Any member of the Jewish community, or their descendants, who lived in Spain and Portugal from the Middle Ages until their expulsion in the late 15th century. They fled first to North Africa and other parts of the Ottoman Empire and eventually settled in countries such as France, Holland, England, Italy, and the Balkan states. They differ from the Ashkenazi Jews in their traditional language, Ladino. There are many Sephardic Jews living in Israel today.

    *Yemenite Jew:* A Jew whose family originated from Yemen.

*Samaria / Shomron:* Samaria, or the Shomron, is a mountainous region west of the Jordan River north of Jerusalem. This area is based on the borders of the biblical Northern Kingdom of Israel. According to today's media, it is roughly corresponding to the northern West Bank. Both "Samaria" and "Shomron" are used interchangeably in this book.

*West Bank:* The West Bank used at times in this book is the equivalent of Judea and Samaria including East Jerusalem. It is a reference to the west bank area of the Jordan River that was taken from Israel during the 1948 War of Independence and occupied by Jordan until liberated by Israel in 1967. The Arabs (Palestinians) are still claiming control of this land, which belongs to Israel.

# Introduction

It has taken me longer to complete this book than I expected, but even so, I believe that what I have written is very important in light of current developments in Israel, the rest of the Middle East, and the world. My prayer is that this book can be widely distributed and read and will have an impact on people who do not really understand the situation in the so-called "West Bank," or so-called "disputed area" of land, in Israel.

I believe that I am the beneficiary of having the unique opportunity of living in Samaria for two years, and of driving to so many parts of the heartland of Israel. I have learned so much about the quality of life in the settlements, the beautiful landscape of rolling hills, valleys, and mountains, and the biblical sites that so many never visit because most tour guides do not include these areas in their itineraries.

Because I have personally learned and experienced so much from this project, even if no one were to buy a copy of this book I would still feel that the whole undertaking was well worth my time. I first visited Samaria with my wife, Charlotte, in 2004 as part of a small, private tour. I must admit that I was a little nervous about touring this area, because I had never before visited the so-called "West Bank" and it was still the tail end of some intifada activity by terrorists. But as a result of that tour my eyes were opened in such a magnificent way to the courage and faith of the Jewish settlers, as revealed in the people we met and the stories we heard.

Since that first visit, I have visited places in Judea and Samaria several times. My wife and I included Shiloh as one of our stops for the See The Bible Tour that we led to Israel in 2005. Also we have escorted a number of our friends to the important sites in Judea and Samaria. Recently because Charlotte was a part of a special study program at Ariel University for visiting scholars during the 2010 to 2012 school years, I had the privilege of living in Ariel, the largest Jewish city in Samaria. It was during this time that I made a decision to write a book focusing mainly on Samaria. The purpose of the book would be to provide a more accurate picture of life in Samaria to counter so much negative and ill-informed media information about the area.

I am greatly indebted to David Ha'ivri of the Shomron Liaison Office who arranged interviews for me with a number of key people who had important roles in the settlement and restoration of the land of Samaria. And of course I am greatly indebted to all whom I met and interviewed. They graciously gave me time out of their busy schedules allowing me to ask questions and gain information about the area.

This book includes biblical and other history of the area as well as a glimpse of how life is lived in Samaria today. It also includes a chapter of significant places to visit that most tours do not include because their location is not considered safe by much of the tourist industry. I have also included an appendix with valuable information of tour guides, websites, and sources of information both for those who would like to visit there and for those who would like to have a part in helping and blessing the Jewish people.

Frank Mecklenburg
May 21, 2013

He struck down many nations and killed mighty kings

— Sihon king of the Amorites, Og king of Bashan and
all the kings of Canaan —

and He gave their land as an inheritance, an inheritance
to His people Israel.

*(Psalms 135:10-12)*

# 1
# Old Testament – Roman Rule

The Bible is the best source document that describes the ancient history of Israel that occurred in the part of Israel known today as Samaria (Shomron in Hebrew). I will summarize the biblical records of the twelve tribes of Israel in the Land of Israel and particularly what happened in the Samaria of today, the biblical heartland and referred to as "The Mountains of God" in the Hebrew Tanakh (Old Testament).

The land known as Palestine, or Israel as is the case with all lands, goes back to the time of creation that shows that God is ultimately in charge. Many Jews believe that the land of Israel was the location of the Garden of Eden. This makes sense when one realizes that there would be no better place for the Messiah to reign from than the place on earth where it all began.

After the Flood, Noah's grandson, Canaan, settled in the land that had once contained the Garden of Eden, even though it was God's plan for Shem's descendants to settle in that same land where He would set up his rule over the earth. This is why the area was known as the land of Canaan when Abraham arrived.

Abraham was a ninth-generation, direct descendant of Shem. He was chosen and sent by God to take over the former Garden of Eden area. In Genesis 13, Abraham and his nephew, Lot, were choosing land where they would settle; the land that Lot chose was described as an area that could have been part of the Garden of Eden.

> Lot looked up and saw that the whole plain of the Jordan was well watered, like the garden of the Lord, like the land of Egypt, toward Zoar. (This was before the Lord destroyed Sodom and Gomorrah.)
>
> (Genesis 13:10)

Could this be a glimpse of what that area was like before the Lord destroyed Sodom and Gomorrah, or was it Lot's way of describing that area?

A few chapters earlier, Noah himself also said:

> Blessed be the Lord, the God of Shem! May Canaan be
> the slave of Shem. May God extend the territory of Japheth;
> may Japheth live in the tents of Shem, and may Canaan be
> his slave.
>
> (Genesis 9:26-27)

From this Scripture we can see that it would be the line of
Shem to whom the Land of God would be given.

Abraham, the great patriarch of Israel, was the first Hebrew
who came to live in Israel. He entered Samaria from the north
and stopped first at the great tree of Moreh near Shechem.

> Abram traveled through the land as far as the site of the
> great tree of Moreh at Shechem. At that time the Canaanites
> were in the land.
>
> (Genesis 12:6)

From here, Abraham viewed the land that God had promised
to his descendants more than four thousand years earlier.

God ordained that Abraham would be in the land, and in
Genesis 23 he became the owner of land by purchasing in Hebron
a burial place for his wife, Sarah, with 400 shekels of silver. As
a result, Abraham and Sarah, Isaac and his wife Rebekah, and
Jacob were all buried...

> in the cave in the field of Machpelah near Mamre (which is
> at Hebron) in the land of Canaan.
>
> (Genesis 23:19)

These are records that cannot be denied. We need to also
remember that all that belonged to Abraham was passed down
to his son, Isaac. And God made it clear that the Land was not
just given to Abraham but to the descendants of Isaac and his
son, Jacob, as well.

> Abraham left everything he owned to Isaac.
>
> (Genesis 25:5)

> And God said to him (Jacob), I am God Almighty; be fruitful and increase in number. A nation and a community of nations will come from you, and kings will be among your descendants. *The land I gave to Abraham and Isaac I also give to you, and I will give this land to your descendants after you.*
>
> (Genesis 35:11-12, italics added)

These Scriptures help substantiate the identity of the rightful owner(s) of this Land. Not only did Abraham purchase land in Canaan, but also his grandson, Jacob, purchased land in Shechem. Jacob paid the sons of Hamor 100 pieces of silver for a place to pitch his tent, about 3,800 years ago.

> After Jacob came from Paddan Aram, he arrived safely at the city of Shechem in Canaan and camped within sight of the city. For 100 pieces of silver, he bought from the sons of Hamor, the father of Shechem, the plot of ground where he pitched his tent.
>
> (Genesis 33:18-19)

Following Jacob's experience in Shechem, the Bible tells us that he moved to Bethel and eventually settled in Hebron, where he was living when he sent his son, Joseph, to check on his other sons who were herding sheep near Shechem.

> So he said to him, Go and see if all is well with your brothers and with the flocks, and bring word back to me. Then he sent him off from the Valley of Hebron.
>
> (Genesis 37:14)

It is quite interesting that both Hebron and Shechem, representing Judea and Samaria of today, are mentioned in the above scripture. The scriptures also provide a record of the transactions and the amounts of the payments. It is incredible that such records are preserved and have been passed down to us today.

## From Moses to the Judges

Moses was chosen by God to bring the people of Israel from Egypt to the land of Canaan. His assistant, Joshua, was chosen to take the place of Moses as the leader of the tribes of Israel. Joshua led the Israelites into the land of Canaan under God's direction, about 1400 BCE, to conquer and cleanse the land from the evil that was so prevalent in that era. In the book of Joshua we find many references to the area of Samaria as the Israelites conquered and settled the Land promised to them by God.

Let us summarize some of these accounts. After they conquered the town of Ai, Joshua built an altar on Mount Ebal. Mount Ebal is just west of Shechem in what is known as Samaria today. It is also next to Mount Gerizim. It is very interesting that Joshua was obeying the Law of Moses by doing this. In the book of Deuteronomy, Moses instructed Joshua to have the people stand on both Mount Ebal and Mount Gerizim as detailed in the verse below:

> When the Lord your God has brought you into the land you are entering to possess, you are to proclaim on Mount Gerizim the blessings, and on Mount Ebal the curses.
>
> (Deuteronomy 11:29)

After Joshua built an alter on Mount Ebal, according to the instructions given by Moses (Joshua 8:30), the tribes were divided with half standing on Mount Gerizim and the other half on Mount Ebal. This was a time for them to read and speak the blessings and the curses given by Moses in the Torah. The blessings were for those who obeyed the Law of Moses, and the curses were for those who disobeyed it (Joshua 8:33).

Some also believe that the Priests and the Levites stood around the Ark of the Covenant in the valley between Mount Gerizim and Mount Ebal, near the town of Shechem, reciting the curses and blessings. The Priests and the Levites might have turned and faced the Mountain of Blessings and recited the blessings, and after each blessing was read half of the tribes standing on Mount Gerizim would shout "Amen." Then the Priests and the Levites would have turned and faced the Mountain of Curses and read the curses while the other half of the tribes, standing on Mount Ebal, would shout, "Amen" after each one.

All of this took place in Samaria. When Joshua was dividing

the land among the tribes, the descendants of Aaron were given the town of Shechem, which was also declared one of the cities of refuge (Joshua 21:21). From this we see without any question that the town of Shechem has belonged to Israel since 1400 BCE. Joshua called for all of Israel's elders, leaders, officials, and judges to assemble in Shechem to address them with a summary of their history, and to call them away from idolatry to serving only the Lord their God (Joshua 24:1-28). Shortly after this special assembly Joshua died and was buried in the land assigned to Ephraim. This great leader of Israel, among many others, is buried in the Land that God gave to Israel.

The book of Judges tells us that Jotham climbed up on Mount Gerizim, the Mountain of Blessings, and shouted a message from there to all the people of Shechem (Judges 9:7). Shechem has always been very important to Israel.

Also, we must not forget that Shechem is where the bones of Joseph are buried. It was at Joseph's request that the Israelites carried his bones out of Egypt and into the Promised Land to be buried in Shechem. Shechem belongs to Israel on the grounds of the purchase of land by Jacob, the use of the land by Joshua and the tribes of Israel, and by the burial place of their ancestor, Joseph. Shechem is also mentioned over and over in the book of Judges.

## Tabernacle at Shiloh

We need to include in this chapter the importance of Shiloh, even though, technically, Shiloh is currently part of Binyamin instead of Ephraim, according to some. Shiloh is located just a few kilometers from Shechem. Shiloh is where Joshua chose to place the wilderness Tabernacle in the Promised Land, and where it stood for 369 years. Probably the most famous reference in the Bible, about Shiloh, is that this is where the prophet Samuel was raised and trained by the prophet Eli before the Philistines captured the Ark of the Covenant around 1100 BCE.

The entire area of what is known as Samaria and Binyamin today has enough Biblical history to substantiate Israel as the rightful owner of the land of the mountains of Israel.

God ruled the people of Shem and the land through the judges and the prophets until He granted the wishes of the people by making Saul, son of Kish, king of Israel. Eventually God replaced Saul with David, whom the prophet Samuel had anointed as King before Saul's reign was completed. Although much land was conquered during the leadership of Joshua, king David conquered even more of the land promised to Israel.

## Kings of Israel

During the reign of king David's son Solomon, Israel built a temple to replace the Shiloh tabernacle, making Jerusalem and Mount Moriah the center of Israel for worship and government. At this time the land under King Solomon's reign extended as far north as Tyre in Lebanon, and as far south as the Brook of Egypt and the Red Sea. It also extended from the Great Sea to the Jordan River, and some distance east of the Jordan as well.

Even after the kingdom of Solomon was divided, with Jeroboam ruling the northern kingdom and Rehoboam ruling Jerusalem and the southern kingdom of Judah, Israel held on to the same land area until the Assyrians attacked and conquered Israel, about 705 BCE. After Babylon conquered Assyria the Babylonians successfully attacked and conquered Judah, destroyed Jerusalem and the Temple, and took most of the Jews captive to Babylon.

## Deportation of Israel and Judah

So, at that point both the northern tribes and tribe of Judah had been taken into captivity. However, this did not mean that there were no Israelites in the Land because some of the poor were allowed to remain.

> But Nebuzaradan the commander of the guard left behind in the land of Judah some of the poor people, who owned nothing; and at that time he gave them vineyards and fields.
>
> (Jeremiah 39:10)

Also, the Assyrians decided to return a Levite, from among those captured, to Samaria so that he could instruct the new residents about the God of the Land.

> Then the king of Assyria gave this order: Have one of the priests you took captive from Samaria go back to live there and teach the people what the god of the land requires.
>
> (2 Kings 17:27-28)

It is important to remember that the land was never empty of all of the Israelites.

## The Second Temple Period

After Persia conquered Babylon, Cyrus, the Persian King, sponsored the return of the Jews to their own land under Ezra and Nehemiah, to rebuild the Temple and repair the city of Jerusalem so that Judaism could be reestablished in the land, during the years 465 to 423 BCE. During this period of time Israel was not a nation, but neither had any alternative nation been established in the same locality. From that time on until 1948, outside powers and governments controlled the region that had been King Solomon's kingdom, with the exception of a period of 65 years of political independence following the Maccabean Revolt, described below.

Alexander the Great conquered Palestine in 332 BCE, which commenced Greek rule that brought paganism to Jerusalem and the temple. This resulted in the Jewish Maccabean Revolt during which the Maccabean brothers led a number of campaigns against the Seleucid government, via guerrilla warfare. This resulted in the establishment of the Hasmonean Kingdom in Palestine in 142 BCE. Following many more years of a war of independence, the Israelites gained political autonomy in 128 BCE that endured to 63 BCE, when the Roman Emperor, Pompey, reached Jerusalem and made Judea a Roman protectorate.

During the reign of the Romans, travel was much easier and Jews spread out more, with the greatest concentration in Syria, western Asia Minor, and Egypt where Alexandria had become a major center of Greek-Jewish culture. Information about Jewish life under Rome can be found in the New Testament, because Jesus lived in Palestine during the time of Roman rule.

Following revolts against the Roman government by the Jews, the Roman Emperor, Titus, destroyed Jerusalem and the Temple in 70 CE. Many Jews were killed and many fled to other areas, including lands that eventually became Armenia, Iraq, Iran, Arabia, Egypt, Italy, Spain, and Greece in order to survive, but again, not all fled. Sixty-two years after the temple was destroyed, Simon bar Kokhba, the Jewish Commander, led a major rebellion against the Romans in 132 CE/AD that was put down by Emperor Hadrian.

Rome continued to rule over Palestine, persecuting both Jews and Christians, until a radical change brought about by the Roman Emperor Constantine I, who legalized Christianity. Constantine's mother, Helena, made a pilgrimage to Palestine and had churches built on the locations of various events in Jesus' life in Judea.

The stronger part of the empire was the Byzantine Empire that still has remains in Israel. During this period the Christians in Israel were very hard on the Jews. They tried to force them to convert to Christianity and kept them from building any synagogues. Yet we know there were Jews still living in Israel at that time, because otherwise there would not have been any Jews for the Christians to persecute.

## 2
# Post-Rome – Israel's Independence

We know that during the times of persecution by the Romans and the Byzantine Christians there were Jews living in the Land. Although this was a very hard time for the Jews, it was not going to get any better for them inside or outside the land.

## Muhammad and Muslims

We also remember that Muhammad was born in Makkah (Mecca) in the western part of the Arabian Peninsula, and not in Jerusalem or in Palestine. He was not a Samaritan or a Bedouin living in what is now Israel. In 638 CE Muslim Arabs invaded and conquered Israel and Jerusalem and the rest of the Middle East, North Africa, Egypt, and Persia. The invasion was bloody for the long-established Christian and Jewish inhabitants and the countryside was devastated. This was the start of 1300 years of Muslim presence in what the Arabs called *Filastin*, an Arabic rendition of the name "Palestina" given to it by the Romans.

Muhammad originally instructed his followers to face Jerusalem when praying, a gesture designed to win support from Arabian Jews. But later, Muslims switched to praying toward Mecca, and the Koran does not mention Jerusalem. In 715 CE, the site from which the prophet was believed to have ascended to heaven on a night journey was arbitrarily associated with Jerusalem, where the Dome of the Rock was built in 687 AD by Caliph Abd al-Malik. Based on this association, the Al-Aqsa Mosque was built on the Temple Mount and the city of Jerusalem became, after Makkah and Medina, the third holiest city of Islam.

The Muslim Arabs ruled Palestine under the system of *dhimmitude*, the rules that apply to non-Muslim populations conquered by *jihad*. There is a myth that the time of Islamic rule was a "golden age" for Jews, and that they were better treated by the Muslims than by the Christians. This myth has been shattered by scholarship that shows continuous persecution of Jews and Christians under Islamic rule. Again I need to emphasize that the Muslim Arabs from outside the country of what is now called Israel invaded the land that I have shown, in the previous chapter, clearly belonged to the Jews before Romans, Christians, and Muslims ruled in that sequence. And it still belongs to Israel.

## The Crusades

The Catholic Pope commissioned soldiers from all over Europe to make crusades to the Holy Land to liberate it from the control of the Muslims between 1095 and 1291 CE. This was a war between the Catholic Church and the Muslims; however, it also included attacks against Greek Orthodox Christians and some Christian groups considered heretical by the Crusaders. On a popular level, the first Crusades unleashed a wave of impassioned Christian fury that resulted in the massacre of Jews that accompanied the movement of the Crusader mobs through Europe, as well as the violent treatment of Orthodox Christians.

On July 15, 1099, after many battles, the Crusaders entered Jerusalem. They not only conquered the city but also massacred both the Jewish and Christian civilians. Following this, several small Crusader States were created, including the Kingdom of Jerusalem in which 120,000 Franks, who were French-speaking Christians, ruled over 350,000 Jews, Muslims, and native Eastern Christians who had remained since the Arab occupation began in 638 CE.

Again, we need to note that – as indicated above – there were still Jews living in Jerusalem at this time. In 1187 after a period of peace, Saladin was able to form a united Muslim front after his successful battle at the Hattin, and was able to defeat the remainder of the divided Crusaders. At that point the Byzantines, who were fearful of the Crusaders, made an alliance with Saladin. The result was that Jerusalem was again in the hands of the Muslims and the Byzantines. Even King Richard the Lionheart, after retaking Jaffa and Akko on the Mediterranean Coast, did not try to recapture Jerusalem.

There were other Crusades and attempts to conquer Jerusalem and other parts of Israel, but what is known as the Sixth Crusade brought Emperor Frederich II to the Middle East, where he made a peace agreement with Al-Kamil, the ruler of Egypt. This treaty allowed Christians to rule over most of Jerusalem while the Muslims were given control of the Temple Mount, including the Dome of the Rock and the Al-Aqsa Mosque.

Frederich married Yolande, the young heiress to the Kingdom of Jerusalem and after her death in 1228 crowned himself as King of Jerusalem. About ten years later, Muslims who were not happy that Al-Kamil had given up control of Jerusalem, regained control of it in 1244. In 1291, during what is called the Ninth Crusade, the Egyptian Mamelukes, who conquered the last of the Crusader strongholds of Akko and Caesarea, removed all the Franks and Christians from Israel.

The Mamelukes ruled over Palestine until 1517, when Palestine was made a part of the Ottoman Empire whose capital was Istanbul. They ruled 400 years, 1517-1918, with only a short interruption of a six-year rule by the Egyptians. However, during the Ottoman rule the first wave of 25,000 Zionists emigrated to Palestine, mainly from Eastern Europe.

## Jewish Population in Palestine – Pre-Independence

However, this does not mean that there were no Jews living in the land before that. In 1882, Baron Edmond de Rothschild of Paris started to financially back the Jewish settlements in Palestine. In 1896, Theodor Herzl, an Austro-Hungarian Jewish journalist and writer, published *Der Judenstaat*, which advocated for the establishment of a Jewish State in Palestine. In 1891 German Baron Maurice de Hirsch, to aid Zionist settlements, founded the Jewish Colonization Association in London. The first Zionist Congress held in Switzerland called for the establishment of a home for the Jewish people in Palestine, and also established the World Zionist Organization (WZO). During the ten-year period of 1904-1914, another 40,000 Zionist immigrants made their way to Palestine.

Some believe that no one lived in the land of Palestine at this time. But certain sources, including Ben Gurion himself, indicate that in 1914 the Jews made up twelve percent of the population. But we need to know what the figures are both for the number of Jewish immigrants and the other inhabitants.

Regardless, even though the number of inhabitants at that time was not sufficient to populate Palestine as heavily as it could be populated, there were Jews living there, including in what is known as Samaria today. An old photograph of Shechem taken 100 years ago, shows that there were very few inhabitants who lived there then, but there are indications that the inhabitants who were there were Jews and not Arabs. Also the news magazine, *Israel Today* had an article in its July, 2011 issue about Arabs who had Jewish backgrounds. They had been forced to convert for their survival many years ago but have not forgotten their roots. This shows us that some Arabs are not Arabs, but Jews. Although these Jews are not in a dilemma about how they would be able to change back to Judaism, it does show that Jews have always been in the land.

In 1867, American author Mark Twain toured the Holy Land and wrote a description of Palestine as a place in ruins and rather desolate.

> One may ride ten miles, hereabouts, and not see ten human beings ... No man can stand here ... and say the prophecy "and your land shall be desolate and your cities waste" has not been fulfilled ... hardly a tree or a shrub anywhere ... Of all the lands there are for dismal scenery, I think Palestine must be the prince ... It is a hopeless, dreary, heart-broken land ... Renowned Jerusalem itself, the stateliest name in history, has lost all its ancient grandeur, and is become a pauper village.[1]

---

[1] Mark Twain: *The Innocents Abroad*, American Publishing Co., 1869. From *Israel Today*, "Israel the Desolation of Exile" by Aviel Schneider, April 2012.

One source says that the population of Palestine in the early 1800s was 350,000, which is not a great number for an area of that size. The same source points out that in 1912 the population had increased to 657,000 Muslim Arabs, 81,000 Christian Arabs, and 65,000 Jews. Indications are that the reason for an increase of Muslim Arabs at that time was the Jewish migration and development in the late 1800s and early 1900s, which attracted many Muslim Arabs from neighboring areas.

The reason for this is that the development in the Land as a result of the Jewish migration opened up many opportunities for employment that had not been there previously. Again, neither Arabs nor Jews were citizens of Palestine at that time because both were living there under the authority of the Ottoman government. There was no local, indigenous Jewish or Arab nation to belong to at that time because the area was still governed by a powerful foreign power.

However, as long as the Ottoman government allowed new residents to buy and develop land, the Jews had the same rights as the Muslim Arabs. The Jews legally purchased land from the local Arabs and had good relations with them, for the most part, until the Arabs were stirred up by opposing parties. It is very important to keep in mind that buying land in another country by outsiders is not at all uncommon. As long as the sale of property between parties is legal and documented, then all people and all governments should recognize it.

Akiva Eldar, in his *Haaretz* website article "Tanks in the Distance," writes about what Yossi Verter wrote about in an encounter that Benjamin Netanyahu had with a CNN reporter in Eilat in 2001. The reporter told Netanyahu that Israel had stolen land from the Palestinians. Netanyahu told her that it wasn't the Palestinians' land, and that before the migration of the Jews there were very few people living there. A short time later, in the *Haaretz* website, Netanyahu himself reiterated the claim that at least half the growth of the Arab population in the country, in the first half of the 20th century, was because of Arab immigration. "Not only did the Jewish pioneering bring with it technological and medical progress and raise the life expectancy of all the population, it also brought masses of Arab immigrants," he said.

This was not new to Netanyahu because the same arguments can be found in the writings of the revisionists, and also in Joan Peter's book, *Time Immemorial,* published in 1984. In the same article Akiva Eldar shows that Middle East historian, Yehoshua Porat, from Hebrew University, claims that there was very little Arab immigration, but that the population growth was a result of natural birth. He says that some Arabs did come from Syria to work for the Jews, but after the work was finished they returned home again. [2]

The truth about the land of Israel and the Jewish people continues to be distorted and changed to try to support making Israel a Muslim/Arab Palestine. We will not to go into a lot of detail here, but I want to summarize history enough to show how all of this has a bearing on Israel and the Jewish right to the land of their forefathers.

## British Rule Over Palestine

A pivotal point in all of this was the start of World War I in 1914. A major factor in making Palestine into a homeland for the Jewish people was the writing of the Balfour Declaration in 1917, by the British Secretary of State, Lord Arthur James Balfour, a year before the British and Allied Forces finished defeating the Ottoman Empire.

In 1918, the 400-year reign of the Ottoman Empire came to a close with Britain as the power in charge of Palestine and the Middle East. The Balfour Declaration clearly stated support for a sizable Jewish home state, which was also supported by Winston Churchill and Prime Minister David Lloyd George who was not known for his love of the Jews.

Following publication of the Balfour Declaration Israel received a mandate from the League of Nations to establish such a homeland, including the West Bank and the East Bank

---

[2]Eldar, Akiva. Haaretz News, July 19, 2001.

# The British Mandate in the Land of Israel. Current-day Israel is only a quarter the size of the original Land of Israel

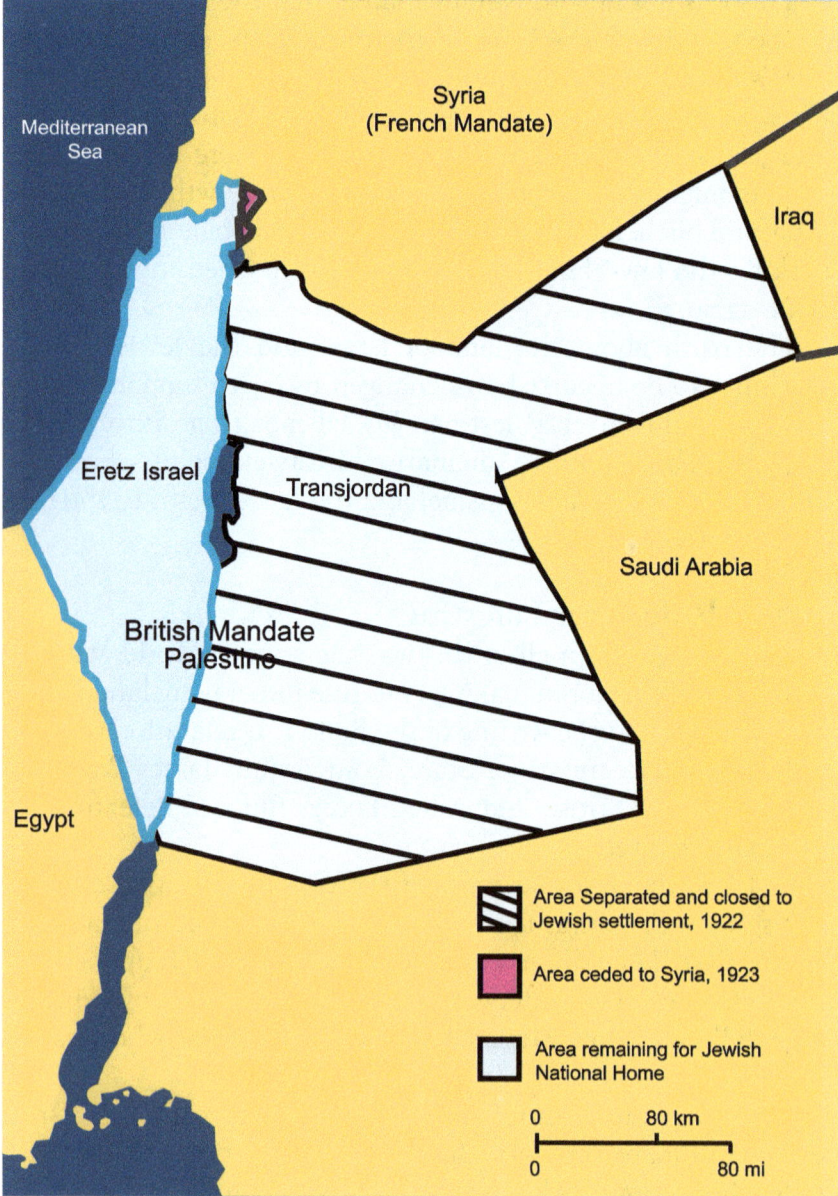

Syria
(French Mandate)

Mediterranean
Sea

Iraq

Eretz Israel

Transjordan

Saudi Arabia

British Mandate
Palestine

Egypt

Area Separated and closed to
Jewish settlement, 1922

Area ceded to Syria, 1923

Area remaining for Jewish
National Home

0        80 km

0        80 mi

© 2003-2010 Koret Communications Ltd. www.koret.com

of the Jordan River. The San Remo Resolution was agreed upon and signed April 24, 1920 during the San Remo Conference, by Great Britain, Italy, Japan, and France. This resolution formally legalized the earlier Balfour Declaration and was to be the legal grounds for administering the Ottoman Empire and establishing a home country for the Jews. But later, in a move that still seems to have been illegal, 74 percent of what had originally been promised to Israel was sliced off. Notwithstanding this great loss, after World War II the United Nations voted that the remaining land would be a Jewish homeland that included what is now called the West Bank.

As the British mandate over Palestine was ending, UN Resolution 181, in 1947, recommended the establishment of two States, one Jewish and one Arab. The Jews accepted this and went on to create the State of Israel, but the Arabs rejected this idea and started a war to destroy the newly established state.

Meanwhile, although it once seemed that the British were in full support of a Jewish homeland, we find that this turned out to not be the case. Nonetheless, between 1922 and 1947 the Jewish population and economic development continued to increase in spite of opposition from the British, who seemed to favor the Arabs more than the Jews, although some in the British military did all they could to support the Jews.

The Jews struggled against both the British and the Arabs. The Haganah, a paramilitary organization became the forerunner of the Israel Defense Force. The Haganah was necessary to protect the Jewish settlers. There was some protection from the British, but not much, and the British were known to provide arms to the Arabs but not to the Jews. According to Ezra Ridgley who was interviewed by Tamar Yonah of Israel National Radio, the fighting and attacks from the Arabs is what led Britain to change its mind regarding a homeland for the Jews and restricted migration of the Jews in the late 1930s and yet opened the immigration for Arabs. This decision possibly kept some three million Jews from escaping death during the Holocaust.

Many who had survived the Holocaust and tried to migrate to

Palestine were placed in a prison camp as soon as they set foot on what was to become their homeland.

## The Birth of the Nation of Israel and the War of Independence

On November 29, 1947, the UN General Assembly voted to end the mandate and to establish two states, but the Arab League rejected this and the very next day, local Arabs began attacking the Jewish community. On May 15, 1948, the State of Israel was officially established by a vote in the UN. Both the Arab uprisings in 1947 and establishment of a Jewish state resulted in the start of the 1948 Arab-Israeli War of Independence. The Jews had no choice but to fight to defend themselves or lose their one-day-old nation that had taken so long to attain.

Sadly, many of the wars and uprisings could probably have been avoided if a Jewish State had been established following World War I.

When we see what the Jewish people were up against just to protect themselves and survive until the UN declared that they were, in fact a nation, all of the above simply shows their determination to survive and have their own country no matter what the cost. Unfortunately, this struggle has never ended and still continues today. Indeed, I expect to see even more determination and fight when it comes to those who are now living in the biblical Heartland of Judea and Samaria.

Areas such as the mountains of Samaria are of more value to the biblical, religious Jews than the coastal areas. In light of what happened in Gaza in 2005 these Jews who are living in Samaria because they know that is exactly where God wants them, will struggle and fight with their lives if necessary to stay where they are.

Unfortunately, at times their struggle is more against their own government than against the Arab Muslims. If only the Israeli government would believe the Bible, stand against the pressures from other nations, and annex all of Judea and Samaria, that would be the solution that God wants to see. What the settlers

## Second Partition, 1947: UN proposes partition - Israel accepts; Arabs reject and go to war

Lebanon

Metulla

Mediterranean Sea

Nahariya

Syria

Haifa

Netanya

Tel Aviv

Jaffa

Jerusalem

Yad Mordechai

Kfar Etzion

Transjordan

Beer Sheba

Egypt

Mandate boundary

☐ Jewish State

☐ Arab State

☐ International Zone

0   40 km

0   40 mi

are doing in Judea and Samaria is no different than what the settlers in Israel did before independence. Those early settlers were brave and withstood strong opposition while working hard to develop the land. At the same time they established protection from those who wanted to destroy them.

## 3
# Israel's War of Independence
# – The Yom Kippur War

After the State of Israel was officially established by a vote in the UN and the Israel Defense Force was formed, there were Arab riots and a blockade of Jerusalem. The fighting escalated and spread throughout Israel. Those still living in the Jewish Quarter of the Old City of Jerusalem were allowed by Jordan to leave, but the Haganah defenders were taken as prisoners to Jordan.

In September, Israel decided to stop fighting Jordan and so forfeited the Old City of Jerusalem. I understand that they did this in order to focus on the need to defend themselves against Egypt. When the war ended, Israel was left with the Galilee, including the west side of the Sea of Galilee, but with Syria in control of the Golan Heights and Mount Hermon. Israel also had the stretch of the Mediterranean Coast from Lebanon to the Gaza Strip, West Jerusalem not including the Old City or the Western Wall (Wailing Wall), and the Negev all the way to Eilat on the Red Sea, including the western side of the Dead Sea.

In 1949, the armistice line at the end of the fighting was accepted as a border, although it did not have any legal status as a border.

> The West Bank is defined by the so-called Green Line drawn in 1949, as the armistice line that ended the military hostilities. No armistice agreement can be construed as a treaty, especially when considering that the Arabs themselves always opposed the adoption of the Green Line as a formal boundary.[1]

---

[1]Benzimra, Salomon (2011-11-10). *The Jewish People's Rights to the Land of Israel* (Kindle Locations 1854-1858). CILR. Kindle Edition.

# Judea & Samaria - A tall mountain range controlling the narrow, low plains of Tel-Aviv

0   40 km

0      40 mi

○ Israeli communities

● Arab communities

Lebanon

Syria

Kiryat Shmona

Safed

Haifa

Mediterranean Sea

Afula
6 mi/10 km

Jenin

9 mi/15 km
Netanya   Tulkarm

Nablus

Kalkilya

11 mi/18 km
Tel Aviv Jaffa

4 mi/6 km
Ben Gurion Airport

Ramallah

10 mi/17 km   Jerusalem

Bethlehem

Ashkelon

7 mi/11 km

Beit Hanoun   Sderot
3 mi/5 km

Hebron

Jordan

Gaza

25 mi/40 km

10 mi/16 km

Beer Sheba

Egypt

© 2003-2010 Koret Communications Ltd. www.koret.com

## Toward Six-Day War, 1967

From 1948, all the way to victory during the Six-Day War, Israel was continually attacked by Syria, which fired rockets from the Golan Heights down on the communities of the Galilee. Egypt continued to control the Gaza Strip while Jordan was in control of the West Bank. If you look at a map of that period you will see that some of the strip along the Mediterranean Sea was a very narrow piece of land only nine miles wide at the narrowest point between the West Bank and the Mediterranean Sea. It takes only three minutes to fly across Israel. Jordan occupied all of the historical biblical land of Samaria and Judea starting in 1949 and until 1967. The Israelites accepted their situation by continuing to build and develop their new nation. For example, Tel Aviv has continued to grow along with Jerusalem and Haifa and other communities.

Demographics have always been a major factor in assuring that Israel will continue as a Jewish democratic nation with a Jewish majority. In the 1930s the Jewish population made up a third of the population of Palestine, but in 1947, the Jewish population increased to about 60 percent of the total by the time independence was granted.

Of the more than 800,000 Arabs who lived in Palestine before 1948, only about 170,000 remained after the War of Independence. In 1945, there were more than 870,000 Jews living in the various Arab states. Many of their communities dated back 2,500 years.

During and after the War of Independence, Jews living in Arab countries near what is Israel today emigrated into Israel from Arab nations because they were forced out of their countries and lost their homes and personal belongings. Throughout 1947 and 1948 these Jews were persecuted. Their property and belongings were confiscated. There were anti-Jewish riots in Yemen, Egypt, Libya, Syria, and Iraq. In Iraq, Zionism was made a capital crime. The Jews arrived in Israel destitute, but they were absorbed into the society and became an integral part of the new State of Israel. They were the true refugees.

In effect, then, a veritable exchange of population took place between Arab and Jewish refugees. The Jewish refugees became full Israeli citizens while the Arab refugees remained "refugees" according to the wishes of the Arab leaders. Even though the UN calls the Arabs in the surrounding Arab countries refugees, only the Jews are refugees according to the UN policy. The definition of a refugee is one who is forced to flee his home country due to war or political action. In this case the Arabs were not forced to leave, but rather left of their own choice because Arab nations told them to leave for three days while they wiped out Israel and then they could return. In some cases the Jews begged the Arabs not to leave. The Arab village of Abu Ghosh in the foothills of Jerusalem was the only Arab village in that area to remain neutral and helped keep a way open for Jews to get supplies through to the besieged Jews in Jerusalem. It is also reported that they hid Jews in their homes. This may very well be the reason that Abu Ghosh continues to succeed and has good relations with the Jews.

According to the Arab leaders, the 1949 armistice line had no political significance. Following the 1948 War of Independence, Jordan was in charge of the West Bank. It seems logical that the UN at that time would have worked toward the establishment of a Palestinian State, but the UN declared that Resolution 181 had no binding authority. The resolution for two states was rejected in 1947; legally that opportunity has been lost.

The so-called Green Line is still referred to as a 1967 border, but it has not been since 1967 – or before 1967 – and it has never been an international border. The 1949 agreed upon borders had to do with Israel, Jordan, Syria, and Egypt and not the Palestinians. Between 1949 and 1967, Israel was attacked by Arab Muslim countries that to this day still do not want to recognize Israel as a homeland for the Jewish people.

In 1956, Egypt refused to permit Israeli ships to use the Suez Canal and blockaded the Straits of Tiran, which erupted in the second Arab-Israeli war, known as the "Suez War." France and the United Kingdom supported Israel in their fight to reopen the canal to all nations. All three of these countries invaded Gaza and the Sinai Peninsula. The United States then led a series of negotiations, and Israel, France, and the United Kingdom withdrew from the Sinai Peninsula after they were guaranteed freedom for Israel and others to have access to the Red Sea and the Suez Canal. Israel also refused to withdraw from Gaza until they were assured that the attacks from there would cease.

It is important to note that in 1963 and 1964 the Arab League established the Palestinian Liberation Organization, with Yasser Arafat as its chairman. This group was behind 35 terrorist raids on Israel in 1965, 41 in 1966, and 37 in 1967, all occurring before the war officially started. Rocket attacks by Syria on the Galilee area, from the Golan Heights, greatly increased in 1965 and 1966 and made things unbearable for the Jews living there.

## Six-Day War, 1967

The Six-Day War was an act of God that cracked open the door for Jewish Settlements in Judea and Samaria. It began with a major threat to Israel in 1967, when Syria, Jordan, and Egypt began preparing for a major attack on them. Several things indicated to Israel that they were going to be attacked. "Egypt's military delegation proclaimed: 'We are confident that we are making fast strides toward the realization of our common goal – the elimination of Israel and full unity.'"[2]

One indication of an impending war came when Egypt ordered the removal of the UN Forces that were serving as a buffer between Egypt and Israel. Also, Egypt had massed 100,000 troops on their border, while Syria massed 75,000 soldiers and Jordan massed 55,000 on their respective borders. Egypt also had 9,000 troops and 200 tanks on the Gaza border itself. They also closed the Red Sea to any Israeli shipping.

Israel knew they were outnumbered and that their only chance for survival would be to get the jump on their enemies. The United States did not want Israel to make the first move,

---

[2]Oren, Michael B. *Six Days of War*. Random House Ballantine Publishing. p. 31.

and told Israel that if they did so Israel could forget about support from the U.S. government. But the U.S. was in a dilemma when it came to dealing with the Arabs and Israel. What we know now is that Egypt was planning to attack on May 27, 1967. Gamal Abdel Nasser, president of Egypt, postponed the attack, which was upsetting to his military pilots, but the sovereign hand of God again protected the Jewish nation.

Yigal Allon, the Israel Labor Minister said, "Does anyone around this table really think that we should let the enemy strike first just to prove to the world that they started it?" Moshe Dayan who became Defense Minister on June 1st, was a realist and was all for striking Egypt as soon as possible. At the same time, Egypt decided that it would be best for them to wait for Israel to make the first move in order to avoid bad press.

I recently learned that the United States had a plan to attack Israel just prior to the 1967 War, for the purpose of protecting Israel and to keep Israel from extending its territory east or south. But the United States did not know about Israel's planned surprise attack on Egypt. Egypt was expecting Israel to attack at dawn on June 5. They had the day right, but did not count on Israel's ability to surprise them.

On the morning of June 5, not at dawn, but at 9:00 a.m., Israel launched Operation Focus, a large-scale surprise air attack that officially began the Six-Day War. Although some accused Israel of starting the war, Israel knew that the buildup of troops along their borders was an indication of a war about to be started by her enemies. The only way for Israel to survive and win was to get the jump on the enemy.

When Israeli planes did not show up at dawn as expected, the Egyptian pilots relaxed and left their aircraft to eat breakfast. The skilled Israeli pilots were then able to fly low enough to avoid the Egyptian radar, and therefore they came in from an unexpected direction and wiped out most of Egypt's aircraft. It is said that within 100 minutes, 13 airbases, 23 radar stations and anti-aircraft sites, and 107 aircraft were destroyed. Israel now had control of the skies. At 10:35 a.m. that morning, Israeli

Chief of Staff Yitzhak Rabin received a report that Egypt's air force had ceased to exist. Their unexpected attack was even more of a success than the Israeli military had hoped for.

Just after the ground war in the Sinai started, Egypt announced great victories when there were none, and the Egyptians began to celebrate in the streets of Cairo. But Egypt no longer had the air power to provide cover for their tanks and they were having trouble with their communications. Israeli tanks surprised the Egyptian tanks because the Israelis learned that by deflating the tires on their tanks they could drive them right across the sand and approach the Egyptians from an unexpected direction. Egyptian soldiers were forced to retreat and Israel wound up in control of the entire Sinai Peninsula and part of the Suez Canal.

Israel then made a deal with Jordan that as long as Jordan did not attack, Israel would not fight them. But when Jordan started shelling West Jerusalem, Israel had no choice but to defend itself. The Israel government did not plan on capturing the West Bank, but because they were forced to defend Jerusalem they unexpectedly captured not only all of the Old City and East Jerusalem proper, but all of Judea and Samaria too.

> First, the Israeli government had no intention of capturing the West Bank. On the contrary, it was opposed to it. Second, there was not any provocation on the part of the Israel Defense Force (IDF). Third, the rein was only loosened when a real threat to Jerusalem's security emerged. This is truly how things happened on June 5, although it is difficult to believe. The end result was something that no one had planned.[3]

Israel also gained control of the Golan Heights from Syria, which eliminated the rocket attacks from those heights following the Six-Day War. Syria claimed they were victorious because Israel captured only a little of their territory, but it was a very important piece of real estate. By the end of the war Israel had control of

---

[3]Louis, Wm. Roger, Shlaim, Avi. *The 1967 Arab-Israeli War: Origins and Consequences*. Cambridge University Press, 2012. p. 47.

## Map of Israel on June 10, 1967

Lebanon

Golan
Heights    Syria

Haifa

Mediterranean Sea

Samaria

Tel Aviv
Jaffa

Jerusalem

Judea

Gaza

Beer Sheba

Suez
Canal

Jordan

Sinai
Peninsula

Eilat

Gulf
of
Eilat

Gulf
of
Suez

Saudi Arabia

☐ Israeli territory
before Six Day War

☐ Under Israeli control
after Six Day War

Egypt

| 0      40 km |
| 0      40 mi |

Red Sea

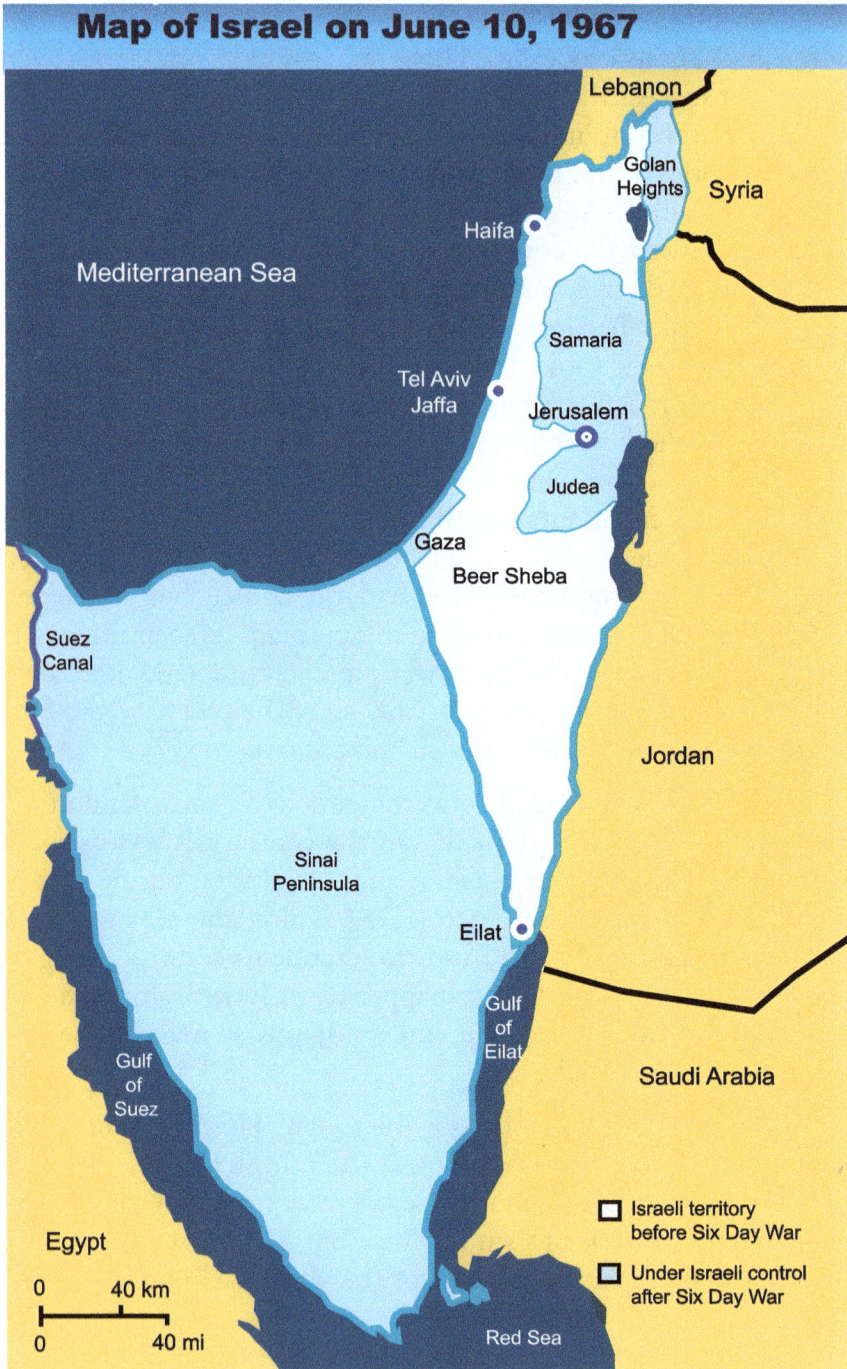

© 2003-2010 Koret Communications Ltd. www.koret.com

the Golan Heights, Judea and Samaria, all of Jerusalem, Gaza, and the Sinai Peninsula. Many considered this war a miracle – clearly, the hand of God was with Israel. However, it was a costly war for Israel, which lost 115 lives recapturing the Golan Heights and 662 lives in other fighting. However, the Arab loss was much greater: 15,000 Egyptians, 2,500 Syrians, and 800 Jordanians.

## Post Six-Day War

Some 350,000 Arabs fled to Jordan to avoid being caught in the crossfire. Also, rumors were spread in Jericho to the effect that all the youth would be caught and killed by Israel. Some fled in fear that they would no longer receive money from their families working abroad. Members of the Palestine Liberation Organization fled to avoid being captured by Israel. Meanwhile, reports of forced deportations by Israeli soldiers seem to be unfounded. On July 2 through September 11, Israel allowed those who fled during the Six-Day War to return to Judea and Samaria as they wished. However, after September 11, they were no longer allowed to return.

At the same time, Jews living across the Arab world faced persecution and expulsion following Israel's victory. Mobs descended on Jewish neighborhoods in Egypt, Yemen, Lebanon, Tunisia, and Morocco, burning synagogues and attacking individuals. In Tripoli, Libya alone, 18 Jews were killed and 25 were injured, while in Egypt 800 were arrested, including the chief rabbis of both Cairo and Alexandria. All their property was confiscated by the government. In other countries there were house arrests and leaders were imprisoned. About 7,000 Jews were expelled from these Arab countries and allowed only one bag for some personal things leaving all their belongings behind.

In November 1967, the UN Security Council adopted Resolution 242, which was supposedly a formula for Arab-Israeli peace that would require Israel to withdraw from land gained during the war in exchange for peace with their Arab neighbors. That has served as the basis for peace negotiations. However, Resolution 242 has two interpretations. One says that the defender has to return land obtained while defending against the aggressor, and the other says that returning land taken during a war applies only to the aggressor and not the defender.

> The Security Council did not say that Israel must withdraw from "all the" territories occupied after the Six-Day war. This was quite deliberate. The Soviet delegate wanted the inclusion of those words and said that their exclusion meant "that part of these territories can remain in Israeli hands." The Arabs also wanted the word "all" included, but that was rejected; they then insisted on reading Resolution 242 with the "all" in it after that was rejected. [4]

When explaining the British position on this, Lord Charadon said:

> It would have been wrong to demand that Israel return to its positions of June 4, 1967, because those positions were undesirable and artificial. [5]

Some say that Israel partially or wholly fulfilled the requirements of Resolution 242 when it gave up the Sinai Peninsula. The peace treaty with Egypt settled that land issue and the peace agreement with Jordan settled the issue of Jerusalem, Judea, and Samaria. July 31, 1988 Jordan ceased to lay any claim to Judea and Samaria although they still oversee the Temple Mount in Jerusalem. At that point Israel would have been wise to annex Judea and Samaria as it did the Golan Heights. Just imagine the lives, houses, money, and time that would have been saved, but that is now hindsight. Now the current situation must be handled in the wisest and best way possible.

What obligations does Israel have with the Palestinians in light of Resolution 242? The Palestinians are not mentioned anywhere in Resolution 242. Nowhere does it require that Palestinians be given any political rights or territory. Almost as many Jews fled

[4] The Meaning of Resolution 242. The Jewish Virtual Library. The American-Israeli Cooperative Enterprise. Copyright 2013.
[5] Beirut Daily Star, June 12, 1974.

Arab countries as Palestinians left Israel. The Jews, however, were never compensated by the Arab states, nor were any UN organizations ever established to help them. We should not be surprised that in 1968 the PLO rejected Resolution 242, even though they had no legal basis to do so.[6]

After the Six-Day War, Ariel Sharon presented a plan that would have dissolved the refugee camps that had been in Samaria and other parts of Israel since 1949. He felt that it would eliminate the problem of people (i.e., terrorists) being bred in those camps. Sharon's plan called for resettling the Arabs in established Arab villages in Samaria and Judea. His plan called for education, decent housing, and integration that would overcome the despair of a refugee camp.

He also felt that another form of goodwill would be to take refugees – especially those in Gaza who were not connected with the PLO and who themselves had suffered at the hands of terrorists – and resettle them in Arab communities in the undisputed areas of Israel, such as Nazareth or Akko. His plan was practical although he felt that the process would take at least ten years to accomplish in the right way. He also told the cabinet that another way to overcome the refugee issue would be for the Arab countries to absorb them.

Sadly, some of these camps are virtual cities today. Technically, refugee camps cannot exist that long. All these years the refugees have simply been pawns in the hands of political interests. Meanwhile, the Arab countries were (and still are) truly obligated to do what Sharon suggested, because Israel absorbed a million Jews who were refugees from the Arab countries. These Arab countries forced the Jews to leave their homes and businesses. But, neither Israel Prime Minister Levi Eshkol, nor Golda Meir, the next Prime Minister, would accept Sharon's plan. As a result, the refugee issue is still with us more than 40 years later.[7]

---

[6]Ibid.

[7]Uriya Shavit, Haaretz News, May 28, 2002.

## Jordan, Arafat, and the Palestinians

King Hussein of Jordan did not want another war for fear of losing even more territory, so he decided not to join this war even though he eventually supported Syria. Anwar Sadat was going to war to help the PLO win control of Gaza and the West Bank. Hussein still felt that the West Bank was part of his kingdom and hoped to regain control again for Jordan, not for the Palestinians.

For this reason King Hussein was not at all happy with Yasser Arafat, who was the cause of the Black September crisis in 1970. During this war between Jordan and the PLO thousands – mostly Palestinians – were killed as Hussein struggled to hold on to his monarchy. Since Yasser Arafat was from Egypt, one can understand why Egypt would fight for the Palestinians. The Palestinians were vying for control of Jordan, bringing a complete change of government. The Fatah did not look at Jordan as a foreign state and the Arabs felt that Jordan was their home country. The present Hashemite Kingdom of Jordan is historically and geographically a part of Palestine.

It is a forgotten fact that Jewish soldiers were the ones who helped the British liberate what is now Jordan, from the Turks, and that this was to be part of a homeland for the Jews. Instead, Jordan is now the homeland of the Palestinians, so they are not without a country, as the widely known myth would have it. The Jordanians did not succeed in destroying Yasser Arafat or the other Fatah leadership, who began to prepare for their next campaign. That same year, Egypt's Nasser died of a heart attack at age 52. This meant the loss of the greatest outside shield for the Palestinians.

Yasser Arafat knew that he was in a weakened state when Nasser died, so he signed another pact with Jordan to the effect that the Palestinians would submit to all the Jordanian laws, and he instructed his followers to dismantle their bases and no longer carry weapons. In fact, if the Palestinians had honored this agreement, King Hussein would not have had a reason to act against them, but some the smaller parties under Yasser Arafat refused to submit to the agreement with Jordan, which caused a renewing of the conflict.

In November 1970, the Jordanian army began confiscating all the Fatah weapons. There were more attacks, and in 1971 Fatah and the splinter groups declared the need for an end to the King Hussein government. They were concerned about the pending peace agreement between Jordan and Israel. After four days of battle in that same year, the Jordanian army dislodged all the Palestinian bases of operation and kept pushing the Palestinian Liberation Organization (PLO) out of Jordan. There was no longer a threat to the overthrow of the Hussein kingdom.

Some of the Palestinians fled to the West Bank and submitted to the Israeli army. King Hussein gradually gave up his desire to regain control over the West Bank. Arafat fled from Jordan to Lebanon, where he was then expelled to Tunis. From there he went to Gaza and eventually to Ramallah, which became his headquarters for the final years of his life. Meanwhile, Jordan continued to threaten Israel if they should expel Arafat back to Jordan. The members of the PLO, who fled into Israel, were the very terrorists who had carried out murderous raids on Israel from Jordan.

This was all leading up to the Yom Kippur War that started on October 6, 1973. Syria really wanted to retake the Golan Heights for military reasons, and to be seen as the dominant military force in the area. Hafez al-Assad would not even consider negotiations until the Syrians had control of the Golan Heights. He was hoping that such a victory would cause Israel to lose Gaza and the West Bank.

Egyptian President Anwar Sadat felt that even a partial victory would change the balance of power. Sadat was also trying to overcome the shame that Egypt was still experiencing over its defeat during the Six-Day War. A victory would give him the popularity he needed in order to make the changes he felt were needed in Egypt. He was ready to go to war even though he did not have Soviet backing.

Israel and other countries did not take Egypt's threat of

war seriously, based on intelligence reports from deliberate misinformation sent by Egypt. There was not a lot of worry about Syria because Israel thought they would not attack unless Egypt did. Even King Hussein's secret trip to Tel Aviv, to warn Israel's Prime Minister, Golda Meir, about the attack, was not taken seriously. Finally, a few hours before the attack Israel started calling up its reserves, which was easier than usual because most of them were at home or attending services in their local synagogue.

## The Yom Kippur War of 1973

The Yom Kippur War of October 6-25, 1973, which lasted 19 days, was what really opened the door for Jewish settlements in Samaria and more settlements in Judea. While Golda Meir was prime minister, a coalition of Arab countries made a surprise attack on Israel on the holiest day of the Jewish year, which that year coincided with the Muslim holy month of Ramadan. Syrian and Egyptian troops crossed the 1967 ceasefire borders. It was surprising that the enemies of Israel would choose such a holy day to start a war, but in some ways it was not a surprise. Anwar Sadat, the Prime Minister of Egypt, had been threatening war for a couple of years while trying to persuade the U.S. government to force Israel to withdraw from all the areas they had gained during the Six-Day War. He said that he was willing to sacrifice a million soldiers to defeat Israel. He based his demands on his interpretation of UN Resolution 242.

There was no pre-emptive attack in this war, even though General David Elasar told Golda Meir and Moshe Dayan that he favored one on Syria. But he was overruled. It was Golda Meir who made the final decision, based on fear that the Israelis would not receive any help from the United States, or others, if they were accused of starting the war. Israel was again greatly outnumbered. In the Golan Heights, 180 Israeli tanks faced 1,400 Syrian tanks, and in the Sinai Peninsula, 450 Israeli defenders with only 290 tanks in the Sinai were up against 100,000 Egyptian soldiers, 1,350 tanks, and 2,000 guns and heavy mortars.

At least nine other Arab States were giving aid to the war against Israel, including Iraq, which transferred a number of jets to Egypt. Lebanon allowed Palestinian terrorists to shell Israeli settlements in the north. Jordan's King Hussein sent two of his best units to Syria, which means that Jordan was in the war too.

Because Israel was caught by surprise, it meant that they were only on the defense and for the first three days, each time the Israeli army tried to attack they were pushed back by Egypt's anti-tank missiles. Israel's army realized that the Egyptian forces were on an aggressive attack so they did not try to penetrate into the Sinai because they needed to build up their numbers. So Israel wisely spent the next six days calling up its reserves and building up its supplies. As all the reserves were called up for the war they were able to repel the attacks against Egypt and Syria.

When Egypt tried to stop the arrival of reservists, Israel shot down 20 Egyptian helicopters. Meanwhile they planned a major attack once the Egyptians moved away from their cover. On October 15, Israeli forces led by Ariel Sharon broke through, crossed the Suez Canal, and were progressing toward Cairo while other units were moving southward all the way to Port Suez. As the Israel army grew stronger it moved deep inside those respective countries. Then the Soviet Union began to resupply the Arabs and rejected an immediate ceasefire, so the United States decided to counter that action by airlifting supplies to Israel.

Egypt was spared a great defeat because of action by the UN Security Council. However, the Security Council took no action when Egypt had the advantage. On October 22, 1973, the UN passed Resolution 338, which called for all parties in the war to cease firing. When the fighting stopped Israel was only 60 miles from Cairo and only 25 miles from Damascus. At that point Israel had cut off and isolated Egypt's third army and was about to destroy it.

In the end, even though the war looked like a success for the Israeli army it was very costly. Many even considered it a failure because of the 2,688 killed and the 7,250 wounded. However, because King Hussein of Jordan did not directly attack Israel, Jordan was not bombed by Israel and there was no combat fighting in the West Bank. But had the war not been stopped, some of these developments probably would have occurred and Israel's victory would therefore have been much greater.

On the other hand, Israel did not lose anything it had gained in the 1967 war. The greatest Israeli loss of real estate after the Yom Kippur War was the Sinai with its Jewish settlements, which happened six years later, in 1979, in return for a peace treaty with Egypt that came about during the Camp David peace talks sponsored by U.S. President Jimmy Carter.

After many Israelis gave their lives in 1967 to gain control of the Sinai, and in 1973 to defend it, the leaders of Israel gave up that land for peace. This was the first time that Jewish pioneers who braved the hardships to develop the land had to leave their homes, synagogues, and business projects. It is also worth mentioning again that – following the Yom Kippur War – Jewish Zionist pioneers began to enter Samaria.

# 4
# History of Jewish Settlements in Judea and Samaria

As we transition from the history of Israel to the history of the Jewish settlements in Judea and Samaria, we must never forget how the Six-Day and the Yom Kippur wars opened the way for these Jewish settlements to begin. During the Six-Day War Israel gained control of all of Jerusalem, plus Judea and Samaria after Jordan had attacked. However, Israel was not very interested in controlling Jerusalem, Judea, and Samaria.

After the Six-Day War Israel could then have annexed all of Judea and Samaria as they did East Jerusalem and the Golan Heights, but for political reasons they did not choose to do this. Although it was not until after the Yom Kippur War that Jews began to settle Samaria, Jews began to settle in Judea in the area of Hebron shortly following the Six-Day War.

## Settling Judea

Hebron has always been very important to the Jews because it is the location of the Tomb of the Patriarchs – Abraham, Isaac, and Jacob – and it also was the seat of David's Kingdom for seven years before he moved to Jerusalem. Hebron today, with an Arab population of 165,000 and a Jewish population of 500, is the city with the largest Arab population in the West Bank.

The Muslims claim a tie to the city because of their connection to Abraham, and include it as one of the four holy cities of Islam because they believe that this is one of the places in which Muhammad stopped on his way to Jerusalem for his final flight. It is an Arab center for quarrying marble and limestone, blowing glass, creating pottery, and growing grapes and figs. It is also the location of a major dairy business.

## Hebron

Hebron has changed hands several times over the years. As noted earlier in this book, Abraham purchased the land from the Hittites for a place to bury his wife, Sarah, as recorded in Genesis 23:3-17. It became the burial place not only for Sarah but also for Abraham, Isaac, Rebecca, Jacob, and Leah. After the destruction of the first temple it then fell into the hands of the Edomites. When the Jews returned from the Babylonian captivity they began living there again.

The Byzantine Empire followed Rome and they lost their hold on Palestine when the Muslims took over the city in the seventh century. Then the Mameluks were there following Crusader rule. In 1187 CE, due to some agreements with the Mameluk rulers, Jews were allowed to return and establish a synagogue in Hebron. The longest rule over Hebron came during the time of the Ottomans, who occupied the known Israel of today from 1516-1917 for 400 years.

The persecution and the expulsions of the Jews from Europe drove many Sephardic Jews into the Ottoman provinces, including the Holy Land. Slowly Jews began to make aliyah, and some Sephardi Kabbalists settled in Hebron. Records show that in 1523 a group of Karaite Jews consisting of ten families lived in Hebron. As a result, in 1540, Rabbi Malkiel Ashkenazi purchased a courtyard and a house of prayer that he converted to the Sephardic Abraham Avinu Synagogue. This structure was restored in 1738 and enlarged in 1864. In 1807, the Jews purchased a sizable piece of land that today serves as Hebron's wholesale market. In 1838, there were 240 Jews living in Hebron who were under French protection until 1914.

After defeating the Ottomans in 1917, the British took control of Hebron. Unfortunately, in 1929 during the British rule, Muslims slaughtered 67 Jewish men, women, and children. But a few hundred Jews survived that attack because of the kindness of their Arab neighbors, who hid them. This shows that not all the Arabs were against the Jews because it seems that some of the Arabs in Hebron had a friendly relationship with the Jews in order to have risked their lives to hide them.

Two years after the 1929 slaughter, 35 Jews moved into the ruins of the Jewish quarter of Hebron, but then were forced by the British to leave Hebron in 1936 on the eve of an Arab uprising, supposedly for their protection. The uprising lasted from 1936 to 1939 and was against British colonial rule and was motivated by opposition to the mass Jewish immigration. The last Jew was a local businessman, who left in 1947. Egypt, followed by Jordan, then took control after the War of Independence. Jordan's control continued until Israel regained control of land taken away from it in 1948.

Following the Six-Day War, David Ben-Gurion, Israel's first prime minister, felt that Hebron should have a large Jewish settlement. The same day that the Israeli troops entered Hebron, the IDF chaplain changed the Muslim mosque into a synagogue by placing a Torah scroll in it and made it possible for Jews to pray and hold services. For a while both Jews and Muslims worshipped in the same building, but when there was more conflict, the Israeli government insisted on the two groups worshipping in separate places. Hebron is currently the only Muslim city in Israel to also have a Jewish community.

In 1968, a group of Jews occupied the Park Hotel to show that they wanted to start a Jewish settlement again. Judy Lev, a social worker in Israel, shared from her university unpublished thesis during a recent lecture in Ariel, about how Rabbi Moshe Levinger, from Petah Tikva, decided to go to Hebron in 1968 after the Six-Day War. He and others felt like the settlement movement should begin in Hebron because of the historical Jewish connections with it. He told his wife and some others, "We are going to go to the Park Hotel – owned by an Arab – to celebrate Passover and have the Seder meal, and then following the Seder meal, we are going to stay." Because it had been so long since the Arab owner of the Park Hotel had had any customers, he was very eager to rent it out to the Jews.

Six weeks after Israel's Minister of Defense had requested it, they left the hotel and moved to an old military compound

*Tomb of the Patriarchs, Hebron.*

overlooking the city. After growing to 120, they had to move again due to lack of space. Even though the government would not give them permission to settle in the Jewish section of the ancient part of Hebron, they did give them permission to settle in an area just outside the town now called Kiryat Arba the home to some 6,000 Jews today, a beautiful settlement. In 1980, they were finally given permission to resettle in the old city of Hebron and now there are 500 Jews establishing a Jewish presence there.

Following this settlement spearhead in Hebron, Judea, 21 more settlements started up in Judea between the years 1967 and 2002. This is another example of the strong motivation and idealism of Jews to resettle Judea. This included Kiryat Arba, Hebron, and Gush Etzion areas.

## Jordan Valley Settlements

Following the Six-Day War another high priority for Israel was the need to protect the eastern border of Judea and Samaria, along the Jordan Valley, which was still very vulnerable to attacks from Jordan. The Labor government, using the Allon Plan, quickly established 20 settlements from Beit She'an to as far south as the

Dead Sea, using both current and former military personnel and civilian personnel to establish agricultural settlements.

The Allon Plan essentially divides the Judean and Samarian mountain range that runs north-south across western Eretz Yisrael into two demographic and topographic sections. The eastern half of the region begins at the Jordan River and rises steeply westward to the mountain ridges of Judea and Samaria – an area that has a relatively sparse Arab population. The western half, which runs from the mountain ridges to the pre-1967 ceasefire lines, known as the "Green Line," holds most of the Arab population centers.[1]

But while some decision makers favored far-reaching concessions, others – "security men," Eban dubbed them – doubted the Arabs' readiness to negotiate and, for strategic and ideological reasons, insisted on keeping most of the territories. In the Cabinet, Yigal Allon led them, as previously. The labor minister – later foreign minister – voted against the Cabinet's June 19 resolution, and lobbied for the creation of Israeli settlements in the West Bank. These would form a new defense line down the Jordan Valley, around Jerusalem and southward to the Hebron Hills, delineating "an agreed, independent Arab State, surrounded by Israeli territory." Though Allon would die, aged sixty-two, in 1980, the "Allon Plan" would remain Israel's unofficial policy until the advent of Rabin's negotiations with Arafat.[2]

In contrast to Judea and Samaria, the area in the Jordan Valley did not have any (or very little) Palestinian population while it was under Jordanian rule from 1949 to 1967. Israeli army personnel, who remained on the army bases after the Six-Day War, were the ones who started most of the settlements in the army bases in the Jordan Valley. These army base settlements were eventually turned over to civilians to be developed into

---

[1] Atlas, Yedidya and Langfan, Mark. Internet article, Rabin's "Allon Plan". 1992.

[2] Ibid.

civilian communities.

The government supported the establishment of the Jordan Valley settlements because they could see the importance of having Jews near the Jordan River as part of a security buffer. These settlements have always had a strong emphasis on agriculture and farming. Because this was also a rich agricultural area, more and more Arabs have moved to and settled in this region over the years. Currently, a person driving through this area will see not only large Jewish agricultural projects but many Arab agricultural projects as well.

## Post Six-Day War in Samaria

Ariel Sharon described the scene in Samaria right after the Six-Day War by telling about his visit to the area. He tells about taking his wife, Lily, to the liberated part of Jerusalem and then to Samaria and Judea.

> All the roads were choked with cars and people, and every place we stopped we were met by an outpouring of love and affection. I had never seen people in such a state of excitement, visiting Jericho, the old cemetery on the Mount of Olives, The Western Wall, all the holy sites that had been closed to Jews throughout twenty years of Jordanian occupation.[3]

He mentioned having breakfast in Hebron, lunch in Jerusalem, and dinner in Shechem all in the same day. A little later, after some travel overseas he again found crowds of Israelis still exploring and discovering places that were such an important part of their heritage, which they had been unable to visit since 1948. This was such a big deal that hundreds of Jews were out visiting the various sites in Judea and Samaria.

Sharon also recognized the strategic need to keep control of the high terrain of Samaria. Even Moshe Dayan had seen the need to move military personnel into these areas, to show that Israel had control, but even though Sharon tried to persuade

[3]Sharon, Ariel. *Warrior*. New York: Simon & Schuster, 1989. p. 206.

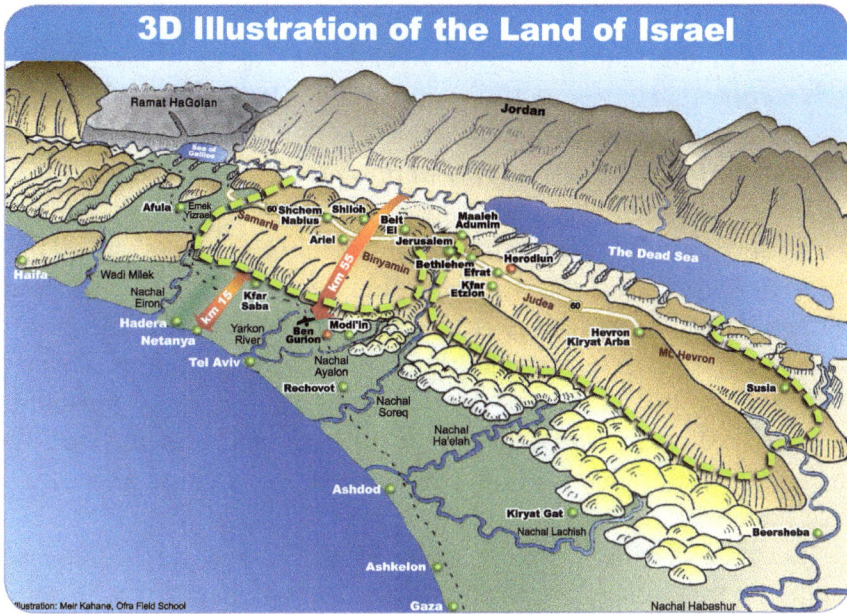

3D Illustration of the Land of Israel

Dayan to let civilian members of the military families also move into Samaria, and to build communities, this seemed too radical to Dayan. Dayan was not willing to take that step.

Some leaders felt that if there were no people and no infrastructure in Samaria then Israel could just walk away from it and not have to figure out a solution to the land and Palestinian issue. To me it seems strange that the leaders were not interested in winning Jerusalem and Judea and Samaria, but it was even stranger that they did not want to keep it. Even at that point they must have been thinking of giving up land for peace. Rabbi Gold, one of my teachers from Karnei Shomron, said that the situation in Samaria and Judea is like playing a game of chess. One player is on the defense while the other is playing to win. And the one who plays to win always becomes the winner.

The plan put forth by Yigal Allon, Deputy Prime Minister, was to secure the Jordan Valley and not deal with the rest. He proposed to make Samaria and Binyamin a demilitarized zone administered by Jordanian civil administration. He was the only one in the government to come up with a plan. However, Sharon pointed out to Allon that Israeli military in the Jordan Valley, and a Jordanian administration over Samaria, would not control the terrorists. He also pointed out that while Jordan had at least six army brigades in Samaria before the Six-Day War they could not control the terrorists, who were a problem for Jordan as well as for Israel.

Unfortunately, hindsight is always better than foresight. Most leaders thought terrorism would decrease since Palestinian terrorists could no longer infiltrate from Jordan, but instead it increased greatly because both Arab countries and the Soviet Union encouraged it. Fortunately, after the Labor government adopted Allon's plan, it was rejected by King Hussein. Had he accepted it, things would have been very complicated and would not have worked.

Because of the strength of the Israeli army, and because so many Arabs had fled to Jordan during the war, security was not a problem until a few years later. It would have been so natural and relatively easy for Israel to annex that entire area right after the war. As the conquering military power they had the right to rule over the land and the people who were living there. They could have determined what land and rights they wanted the Arabs to have, and that would have settled it. There would not have been any issue of so-called "occupation." The door would have been wide open for the Jewish settlers who wanted to move to the area of the biblical heartland. Also, it would have been fairly easy to enforce the laws so that any Arab who was not happy to live under the conquering army would be exiled from the country. The result would have been peace and full development of the area.

A few months after writing this last paragraph, I read David Rubin's book, *Peace For Peace*, in which he suggests his idea of a peace plan. "There can only be a one-state solution in the land of Israel with Israel as the only sovereign nation in that one state." David advocates "an intensive loyal citizenship training course for those who want to acquire membership in a Jewish state." Those wanting to be citizens of the state of Israel would have to prove their allegiance.[4]

Credit has to be given to Sharon for what he did in spite of the opposition he experienced.

> As director of military training, by 1968 I managed to occupy almost every single one of the old Jordanian military bases and police outposts outside the cities. These were in all the most important strategic locations, because the Jordanians in occupation of Samaria and Judea had also had strategic considerations and had built their bases accordingly.[5]

## Toward Settlements in Samaria

Many times when the term "Samaria" is used, it refers to both the Samaria Regional Council and the Binyamin Regional Council. Also, "Samaria" is usually used in contrast to Judea. Binyamin is the area between Samaria and Judea, or the area north of Jerusalem. Judea is south of Jerusalem.

The process of starting new settlements in Samaria was similar to that of Judea. Many Jews with a passion for Judea contributed their strength and energy, believing that it was God's timing for new settlements to be established. Once the door opened up in 1967, without hesitation the pioneers moved ahead. We will see that some of the pioneers in Judea also used that experience to become leaders of the settlement movement in Samaria.

However, it was not until after the Yom Kippur War in 1973 that the settlement movement of Samaria began to take shape. In 1975, at the same time as the starting of the first settlement of Kedumim in Samaria, a very similar thing was going on in Binyamin south of Samaria. The Ofra settlers began by first occupying a former Jordanian army camp.

In Ariel Sharon's biography he describes some of the struggles the nation had in starting settlements in order to populate Judea and Samaria. Right after the Six-Day War in 1967 the border

---

[4]Rubin, David. *Peace For Peace*. Israel: Shiloh Israel Press, 2013. p. 209.

[5]*Warrior*, p. 210.

# Map of Biblical sites: Judea and Samaria: The Land of the Bible

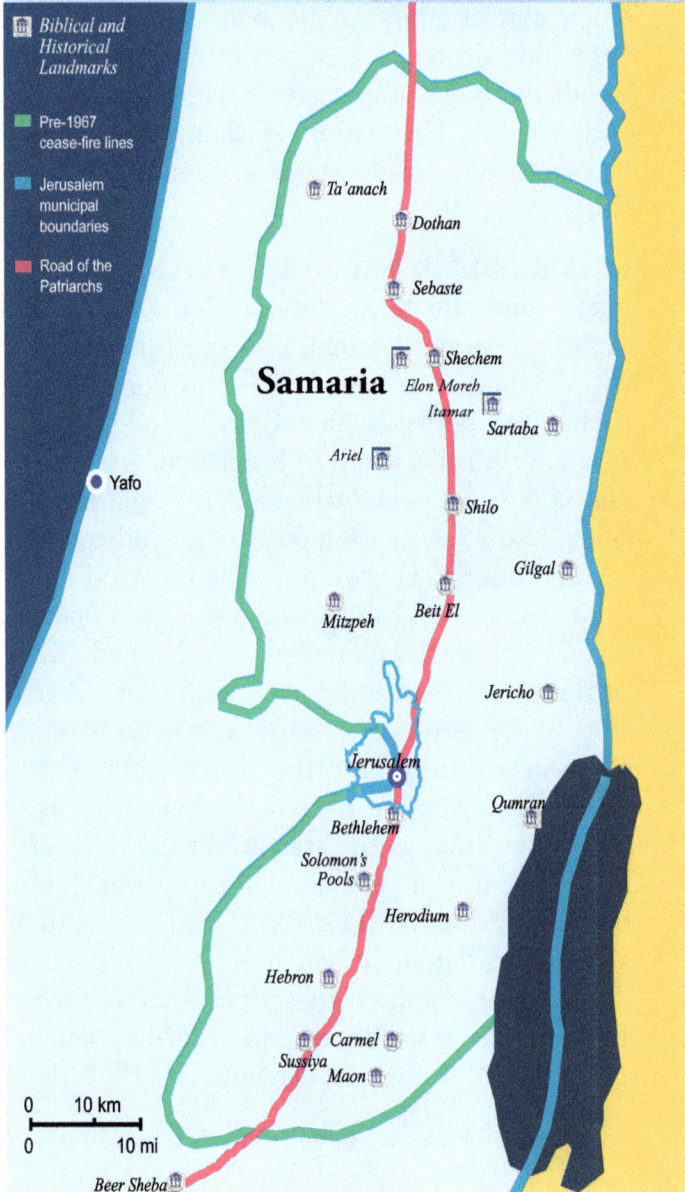

Biblical and Historical Landmarks

Pre-1967 cease-fire lines

Jerusalem municipal boundaries

Road of the Patriarchs

Ta'anach

Dothan

Sebaste

Shechem

Samaria

Elon Moreh

Itamar

Sartaba

Ariel

Yafo

Shilo

Gilgal

Beit El

Mitzpeh

Jericho

Jerusalem

Qumran

Bethlehem

Solomon's Pools

Herodium

Hebron

Carmel

Sussiya

Maon

0    10 km

0    10 mi

Beer Sheba

© 2003–2010 Koret Communications Ltd. www.koret.com

was open, with no barbed wire fences and no longer was there any marked, physical border between Israel and Jordan, as it was before the Six-Day War. On the west side of the Green Line, near Samaria, were a number of well-to-do Arab communities, and also a number of Arab communities just east of the Green Line. There was no difference in the culture, language, or social structure of these communities. Thus the reality of a "Green Line" became more and more fuzzy because there was a mixture of Israeli Arabs and Arabs who were formally under Jordan's rule. The result of the war naturally dissolved borders for a period of time. Israel had a concern about adding so many more Arabs to Israel's population, changing the demographics that might cause the Jews to lose their majority in their democratic nation.

> Another bigger problem in this area were the Samaritan and Judean hills that dominated the coastal plain. The vital strategic issue here was how to give depth to the coastal plain, and how to keep the dominant terrain in our hands now and in the future so that it could never be used militarily by anyone else.[6]

Sharon and others felt that the answer to the problems he identified above was to build both urban and industrial settlements on the high areas overlooking the plains. This would be a strategic move that would not affect any of the rich Arab agricultural land in the valleys. Instead the Jewish communities would be on the high rocky ridges and mountains unfit for agriculture so Arabs would not populate them. And as Sharon suggested, his approach has provided more strategic protection for the western plain.

Another issue after the war was the situation in the Jordan Valley, which was the new border with Israel's neighbors to the east. As mentioned earlier the government established settlements all along the Jordan Valley before any settlements were started in Samaria. According to Sharon and others, this was not sufficient for security and that is why they pushed for

---

[6]Ibid, p. 357.

populating the mountains of Samaria. The plan called for building several roads from east to west as well as establishing settlements. Although there were some roads in Samaria, there were virtually none in the higher terrain. Even Sharon and his team had to walk the higher areas.

> That meant trekking from place to place and climbing with map in hand to decide where each of those settlements would be sited. The days were long and exhausting, clambering up those hills, on foot.

Sharon and others had to try to determine which was state-owned land and which was private. Generally state-owned areas were determined to be what had belonged to the Turkish government during their 400-year occupation, then passed to the British under their 30 years of occupation, then on to the Jordanians under their 19 years of occupation. [7]

## Israel Government and Land Issues

After the government of former Israeli Prime Minister Menachem Begin was formed in 1977, land ownership became an even more complicated issue for Israel. The previous Labor government had been willing to use Arab-owned land, but Begin felt very strong about not taking any land from the Arabs. According to his government, if Arabs were squatting on state land and had cultivated it, then it was off limits for Jewish settlements. This required the use of photos of the land before 1945 to determine the status of the land. Arab-owned land in the West Bank is privately owned. This is in contrast to state land that was owned by the government of Jordan during its occupation of the West Bank.

Adding fuel to the fire, a number of Jews felt that Israel's leaders should immediately give up its control of all land taken during the Six-Day War. In spite of this, the settlement movement continued to develop with the building of roads and the installation of utilities. The settlements in the strategic

---

[7] Ibid, p. 360.

areas were initially started with people living in tents or a few caravans.[8] Even though Prime Minister Begin had strict ideas about state and private land, his view was that all this area should be a part of the land of Israel, which encouraged the growth of the settlements during his government. Another important factor was the appointment of Ariel Sharon as the Minister of Agriculture. But no matter what the government policy was, the settlement movement depended on rugged pioneers who were willing to make the sacrifices to live on barren hills and ridges among a rather hostile local population.

Another event that propelled Ariel Sharon into even more action, in 1979, was the pending peace agreement between Egypt and Israel brokered by U.S. President Jimmy Carter. It is still hard to believe that after Israel's miraculous victory in the Sinai during the Six-Day War, and after sacrificing so many lives of young Israelis to retain control of it during the Yom Kippur War, Israel would give it all up soon and so easily in order to have a peace agreement with Egypt.

They not only gave up the Sinai, but also gave up more than 20 settlements and two towns. Some of the reason for this decision can be seen in this quote from Ariel Sharon in his book, *Warrior*:

> As far as I was concerned, there were only two possibilities: Either establish a close-knit belt of strong populated settlements or give up the settlement idea altogether and look for a different concept. There was no question that the settlements we already had there would not be able to survive by themselves and that they would expire under protracted unpleasant conditions. At the same time I felt strongly that we had to try the experiment of peace with Egypt. I knew that abandoning the existing Sinai settlements would bring an outcry from many in Israel, but after 30 years of existing in a state of war, the question of whether we could make

---

[8]Known as a mobile home in the U.S.A. Mobile home will be used in the remainder of the book.

peace with an Arab state and then live in peace with them was historic. The opportunity had to be taken, even though the risk was great. It was for this reason – and only because Sinai was not part of the Land of Israel – that I supported Begin consistently in his negotiating position and that I voted in favor of the agreement he finally achieved.[9]

This quote gives us the reasoning behind the agreement to give up the Sinai. We must remember that this is what Sharon himself – one of the warriors of the wars – said. After all the struggles he and his troops experienced, and given the memory of all who had fallen during the war, he could still sign the agreement. Perhaps this was the forerunner of the expulsion of Jews from Gaza in 2005.

Sharon knew that after the treaty was signed by Anwar Sadat, President of Egypt, that Sadat would pressure the world powers to insist that Israel give up its control of Judea and Samaria. As a result of this, Sharon said that he helped establish 64 settlements in four years in Judea and Samaria. Some these were barely started, and the living conditions were considered difficult with people living in tents with no electricity or water at first.

The sight of these people washing their babies outside in the cold would bring shivers to my spine. But living near places like Shechem, Shiloh, or Bethel, with their rich spiritual and historical associations, held a meaning for them that translated into joy as well as into utter determination.[10]

## Settlements in Samaria

The establishment of settlements in Samaria grew out of a movement known as *Gush Emunim* group (Block of the Faithful), a national religious movement with the aim of populating the land with Jewish settlers. This movement in Samaria first took over the Sebastia, an abandoned Turkish railroad station, located just outside the Arab village by the same name, not all that far

---

[9]Ibid, p. 396-397.
[10]Ibid, p. 366.

from the ancient city of Shechem, known today as Nablus where the bones of Joseph are buried. The goal of the movement was and is to have a Jewish presence right in Shechem. I will give more detail about the start of the first settlement, Kedumim, but following the establishment of Kedumim, in 1975, two additional settlements, Karnei Shomron and Shavei Shomron, started in 1977.

Karnei Shomron was the second settlement started in Samaria and now has a population of about 7,000. In 1991, the communities of Ginot Shomron, Neve Menachem, and Alone Shilo merged with Karnei Shomron to make one larger community, now with its own governing body. Shavei Shomron started just a little later in 1977. Also, in the same year the settlement of Mevo Dotan was started in northern Samaria.

More and more young Jews from other parts of Israel and many new immigrants were motivated to settle in Samaria because of their Zionism, based on their Jewish heritage.

The Ottoman Turks had built a railroad that came all the way to Shechem through Sebastia from the Jezreel Valley. The remains of the old train station can still be seen, but no tracks are left because – once the train stopped running – the Arabs used the iron tracks for building materials. Sebastia is also the location of the ruins of the capital of the Northern Kingdom of Israel, built by King Omri, the father of King Ahab. In 2002, the Israeli government built a West Bank barrier around the settlement. The residents were not happy about this because they feared that it might become a permanent Israeli border given some kind of two-state solution.

Three other settlements were started in 1978, including Ariel (which is now a city), Kfar Tapuach, and Ma'ale Efraim. Ariel has grown into the largest city in Samaria and the home of Ariel University with a population of 20,000, but originally many settlers expected the first settlement, Kedumim to become the large city.

According to the records kept by the governing councils, only Salit started in 1979, while Elon Moreh and Ma'ale Shomron

*Columned street of Sebastia.*

started up in 1980. Elon Moreh was the original name of the Kedumim group, but the community of Elon Moreh is separate from Kedumim and is directly east of Shechem. Even though the Jews have not been successful in establishing a settlement in Shechem, at least there are Jewish settlements surrounding it as a partial fulfillment of their original dream of settling right in Shechem itself. However the dream has not been completed and will not be completed until they can take up residency there.

Jews in Samaria feel that they have as much right to have a settlement in Shechem as the Jews in Judea who are living in ancient Hebron. It is amazing that as of now the settlements of Shavei Shomron, Mitzpe Yishai, Havat Gilad, Har Bracha, Yitzhar, Itamar, and Elon Moreh all surround the ancient city of Shechem.

From the above we can see that there was tremendous motivation for the Jewish people to settle in Samaria. The growth continued, and a record number of seven settlements started in 1981, which included Hinanit, Einav, Yakir, Beit Aryeh-Ofarim,

Reikhan, Shaked, and Barkan. The expansion also continued with three more settlements added in 1983 – Har Bracha, Alei Zahav, and Sha'arei Tikva. Another big boom started in 1984, adding five more settlements – Itamar, Migdalim, Hermesh, Peduel, and Kiryat Netafim. From 1968 through 1984, the number of settlements in Samaria and the Jordan Valley totaled 38.

From 1984 through 2002, 14 more settlements were started. They included Alfei Menashe, Nofim, Tzofim, Avnei Hefetz, Rachelim, Revava, Tel Dotan, Havat Yair, Tal Menashe, Mitzpe Yishai, El Matan, Bruchin, Nofei Nehemiah, and Havat Gilad. The number keeps growing in spite of the Israeli government's opposition and carrying out some demolition of homes. Usually a new settlement is started in response to a terrorist attack.

## Relationship Between Jewish Settlers and Arabs

In the early days of the settlement movement in Samaria, relations with the Arab people were fairly good. People in places like Elon Moreh and Itamar could drive into Shechem, called Nablus by the Arabs, for shopping and business and feel so safe that they would even leave their cars unlocked. Jews also drove into Ramallah for shopping without any hesitation. According to Daniella Weiss, the establishment of a Jewish settlement in Samaria did not bother the Arabs. In fact, the Arabs were helpful in allowing the Jews to shop in their towns, and by sharing tips about agriculture in the mountains. The leader of Hinanit, Hanan Niv, told us that they have good relations with the Arabs and have provided electricity to their villages. The early settlers of Ariel and other places shopped in Arab villages for fruit, vegetables, and other food items.

During the early years the Arabs eagerly contacted Jews about selling their property. Agreements were made and the transactions were legally recorded. Arabs who worked for people such as Moshe Zar, one of the early Jewish settlers, (more detail in the next chapter) would contact other Arabs about his wanting to buy land, and the result was that Arabs would seek out Moshe in order to sell him land for a good price. However, any Arab who would sell land to a Jew today will be threatened with death.

During the same early years, many Arabs worked for Jews because they were eager to earn money and in fact that continues to this day. In many respects it seemed like a comfortable relationship between the Jews and the Arabs. However, I do not want to make it sound as if there were no problems, but if we were to contrast that period with how things are today then those earlier times could be classified as peaceful by comparison.

## Yasser Arafat and PLO Developments

At the first-ever Arab states summit, in 1964, the Arabs started the Palestine Liberation Organization (PLO) for the purpose of establishing an independent state for the Palestinians. When Yasser Arafat came on the scene and became the PLO leader in 1969, he became active in promoting a Palestinian state and relations with the Arabs began to deteriorate even further. In the early seventies, when Arafat realized that taking over Jordan was a lost cause he began to push harder for a Palestinian state in Judea, Samaria and Gaza.

However, the fact that the Palestinians expelled Arafat from Lebanon shows that not all Palestinians were in agreement with him. What a shame that in 1980 Yasser Arafat had nothing better to do than to rebuild the faltering Fatah, with financial help from Libya, Iraq, and Saudi Arabia. This led to the start of the first intifada in 1987, which included terrorist attacks against the Jews accused of occupying Judea and Samaria. If it had not been for Arafat and those attacks, there probably would still be a reasonable relationship between the Arabs and the Jews. Arafat was able to build on rumors about Israel to stir up a Jihad against settlers and Israel in general, which continued the intifada through 1993.

Most of the attacks were organized by Khalil Ibrahim al-Wazir, nicknamed Abu Jihad, who was one of the Arabs who fled their homes in Israel in 1948. He was the founder of the Fatah Party and so worked very closely with chairman Yasser Arafat as his right-hand man. All of this also had a very negative effect on the relationship between the Arabs and the Jewish settlers. Most of the Palestinians viewed Abu Jihad as a martyr for his actions against the Jewish settlers, who supposedly were occupying Samaria and Judea when – according to the Palestinians – they shouldn't have been there at all.

The world gave Arafat a lot of attention and support because, by the time he entered the picture, the Arabs were being seen more than ever as victims. In the late 1900s, Arafat managed to conduct secret talks with the Israeli government that then led to high-level peace talks. In 1993, they resulted in what was called the Oslo Accords, which stated that the Palestinians were to have self-rule in some parts of the West Bank, and that there was to be an immediate halt to starting new Jewish settlements and the gradual removal of Jewish settlements already established.

However, before this was signed Arafat signed two other letters, one denouncing violence and the other one officially recognizing Israel. In return Israeli Prime Minister Yitzhak Rabin officially recognized the PLO. This was a major factor in what followed, for the next year Arafat, Rabin, and Peres were all awarded the Nobel Peace Prize.

Most of the Arabs in the West Bank accepted the Oslo Accords, however, many refugees and other Palestinian groups did not. Following the signing, Arafat said that he needed lots of money to further develop the Palestinian Authority in the West Bank and Gaza. His main source of funding, he assumed, would be the Gulf Arab States, but they refused to fund him due to his sympathy for Saddam Hussein during the Gulf War.

So, in 1994 he moved to Gaza and became the commander of the Palestinian Liberation Army and the speaker of the Palestinian Liberation Council, both part of the new Palestinian National Authority. What was really significant to Samaria was that Arafat took the liberty of replacing the leader of Shechem (Nablus) with his own appointed man. He felt that the leader of Nablus was not radical enough and was too friendly with the Jewish Settlers. He was determined to fill all the various leadership positions with men who were loyal to him. In this way he could stir the Palestinians against Israel and the settlers.

As a result the Palestinians became even more hostile toward Israel. The second intifada, 2000-2005, resulted in many suicide bombings in many parts of Israel, including Jerusalem, and also against settlers in Samaria and other parts of Judea. But during this terrible time of suffering the settlers remained strong and the settlements continued to grow. We have already listed those that were started during this time, by pioneers who really knew in their hearts that this is the biblical heartland of Israel, and that this land belonged to their ancestors because God had given it to them.

In closing this chapter I want to quote from Avi Zimmerman who wrote the following tribute to Ariel Mayor, Ron Nachman:

> As a member of Knesset from 1992-1996, he fought the Oslo Accords vehemently, warning that signed agreements did not amount to shalom among peoples. He knew his Arab neighbors well, and he feared that they could be overcome by newly empowered political arrivals, who would undermine traditional leadership structures while dismissing the local ethos that predated them. Indeed, a difficult season arrived. The first intifada brought an end to Saturday shopping sprees for Ariel's residents in Salfit's colorful markets. Though Israeli hummus and pita in Ariel were decidedly inferior, it was worth the sacrifice when the alternative was an uncertain dance with death. Needless to say, the bullets fired at Ariel's civilian population during Yasser Arafat's second intifada did little to restore Ron's hopeful shalom.[11]

---

[11]Zimmerman, Avi. *Ron Nachman Says Shalom*. Your Middle East, February 3, 2013.

# 5

# Samaria Settlement History and Pioneers

In this chapter as I write in more detail about the history of the settlements in Samaria, which is the focus of this book, I will bring in the stories of some of the pioneers who devoted their lives to the renewal of the biblical heartland of Israel, of which Samaria is a major part. I have not included all of the history makers, but have included the following: Benny Katzover, Daniella Weiss, Ron Nachman, Moshe Zar, Professor Hillel Weiss, Avri Ran, and Yigal Cohen-Orgad.

## Benny Katzover

As mentioned in the previous chapter, the history of Samaria really began in Judea with people like Benny Katzover who "was one of the major forces behind the return of people of Israel to the hills of Judea and Samaria (Yehuda and Shomron)."[1] He was born in Israel in the town of Petah Tikva and in 1947 served as a security guard for the Jewish settlers in Hebron. He was a university student who took time from his schooling to be a part of the Jews' return to Hebron in Judea after the Six-Day War.

The following quote about Benny Katzover's experience in Hebron in 1968 reveals some of his character, which is also true of most of the settlers.

*Benny Katzover.*

Benny and his friends decided that it was important to explore their rediscovered frontier. They bought a book written by Matan Vilnai's father

---

[1] Goldsmith, Moshe, *The Story of Benny Katzover*.

about *Yidiot Haaretz* (Facts of the Land). They wanted to know about other places in *Chevron* (Hebron) besides the Tomb of the Patriarchs.

After reading about the gravesite of Yishai, Benny decided to check out the place. He followed the map and arrived at the site. Through the gate he saw an Arab hammering away at a rock. Benny waved hello as he entered the area and made his way to the gravesite. After finishing his prayer, when he was leaving, he was stopped by the Arab. The Arab told him that he was a sculptor and showed him the work he was doing. He even treated him to a cup of coffee.

After about an hour Benny finally left the site and returned to the hotel. He was so excited about his discovery that he shared the experience with his friends. He told them that they too must see it. He explained to them how to get there, and they set out on the mission. About an hour later they returned looking pretty upset. Benny asked them what had happened and they told him that an Arab threw them out. Benny couldn't believe it. He decided to personally escort them to the site.

When they arrived, Benny walked in the very same way he had when he first came. He waved hello to the Arab sculptor and led his friends to the gravesite. When they finished, the Arab sculptor, now a great friend of Benny, greeted Benny with a hug. He invited Benny and his group to sit down to a cup of coffee. After they finally finished the meeting and walked out, they were totally blown away. They asked Benny, "How is it that this Arab treated you with so much respect? He's the one that threw us out." Benny asked them how they had entered the site. They said that when they arrived at the gate they were hesitant to enter. The Arab sculptor was looking at them and they asked permission to go inside. He refused, and threw them out. Benny explained that he, on the other hand, had acted as though he was boss and left his fears outside the gate. He had learned a great lesson about how to deal with his new neighbors.[2]

This prepared Benny to be one of the members of the nucleus of Jews who were determined to start a settlement in either Judea or Samaria. This nucleus group is called a *garin,* which literally means "pit of a fruit" or the beginning of something very small that would grow into something very large. Because the term *garin* is used so much in Israel, I will use it in this book to refer to a small group of Jewish settlers. Sometimes I will use the term like it is part of the name of a settlement.

Each nucleus of Jews or *garin* had their site for a settlement at a different location. There ended up being many *garins* or in Hebrew, the plural is *garinim.* I hope this is not too confusing. I have taken the time here to explain this because I use these terms a number of times in this book. The sum total of all of these *garinim* that were part of the settlement movement, known as nucleus groups, were part of the *Gush Emunim,* "block of the faithful", who made up the movement that established Jewish settlements.

Benny Katzover and Rav Menachem Felix had a strong feeling about the area of land where Abraham first set foot and that this land was waiting for Jewish settlers. They also sensed that Joseph, who is buried on a piece of land purchased by his father Jacob, was waiting for the return of his brothers.

In 1972, a year before the Yom Kippur War, Benny and Felix formed a *garin* whose goal was to claim a hilltop in Samaria.

In just a few months the leaders of this *garin* included a pioneering group of 15 families and a group of 15 singles, whose goal was to start a settlement in Shechem (Nablus), the burial place of Joseph. They felt that this was the place to begin the renewal of Samaria because their motive was like that of the pioneers who settled in Hebron just after the Six-Day War. Both Hebron and Shechem are holy sites to the Jews, because both are burial places of the Fathers.

During an exploratory trip in Samaria, one of the places where

---

[2]Goldsmith, Moshe. *The Story of Benny Katzover.* Internet, p. 5.

they considered placing the first settlement was on Mount Kabir, which is the mountain that many feel is the first mountain in the land on which Abraham stood to first view the land that God had promised to him and his descendants. Some also think this might have been the Mount Gerizim of the Bible. The settlement of Elon Moreh today is located at the base of Mount Kabir.

As a followup move they talked with a conservative General, Rehavam "Gandhi" Ze'evi, about establishing a settlement. General Rehavam had been a platoon commander in the IDF in 1948, and from 1964 to 1968 served as Chief of the Department of Staff. While he was in charge of the Shomron (Samaria) after the Six-Day War, he showed the settlers a plan for a Jewish settlement near the ancient city of Shechem, near the current settlement of Itamar. But he told them that if they were to make such a move without government permission he would act without hesitation to remove them from the Shomron. He was known to have removed settlers in 1969 when the Betar group tried to start an unauthorized settlement on Mount Gerizim.

Betar, whose name comes from the last fort to fall during the Bar Kokhba Rebellion, is a paramilitary group that fights those around the world who are against the Jews. The Betar was founded by Ze'ev Jabotinsky in 1923 and was active in fighting against the Nazis in World War II. Jabotinsky was concerned about attacks against the Jews in Galilee in the early 1900s and is known to have said that the best answer to threats and attacks in Israel would be the creation of a Jewish state that would include all of Palestine and Jordan. He also proposed creating Betar to train for military action against all enemies of Judaism.

## Daniella Weiss and the First Settlement – Kedumim

It is no accident that one of the leaders of the settlement movement after the Yom Kippur War was Daniella Weiss, an avid Zionist. Her idealism came down to her from her parents and grandparents, who were also ardent Zionists. Her call in life was to continue preparing the Land for future generations to come. She saw the settlements and Jewish communities in Samaria as merely stepping stones to the real goal of preparing the Land for the Messiah and his people.

Daniella, Benny Katzover, and others became active after the Yom Kippur War in rallying interest in the settlement movement for Samaria and Binyamin. Daniella said that she was changed on one particular day during the Yom Kippur War when she heard the sirens going. This served as a wake-up call to her and other people of Israel, who had previously thought

*Daniella Weiss.*

of Israel as places like Ashdod, Bat Yam, Tel Aviv, Netanya, and Haifa. She realized that God wanted the people to see that these two wars were not just military exercises, but showed that something needed to be done for all of the important biblical sites and for all of the Land given to the people of God.

The Six-Day War miraculously opened the way for the Jewish people to return to Judea and Samaria, and the Yom Kippur War allowed the Jews to continue to hold that Land. Also, it was the Yom Kippur War that God used to initiate the settlement movement in Samaria. Daniella says that although many people try to lessen the importance of the Six-Day War, it was the war that showed that the God of the Bible is still watching over Israel.

Daniella felt that she had a personal call from God after her Yom Kippur experience. She feels that God was saying, "Stop your ordinary life, your Tel Aviv life, and go to the mountains of Samaria and redeem and settle the Land." She began to speak about her desire to see Samaria filled with Jewish people again, and discovered that God was speaking to many others beside herself and was calling them to join together. She began to hold meetings and rallies to raise support. She and her husband eventually joined the group that started Kedumim, the first settlement, in 1975 in Samaria. Kedumim has a current population of 5,000. She feels that even though there are both religious and non-religious people in the Zionist movement, it is the idealism of the religious that has propelled people into Samaria. Religious people, in faith, made the decision to leave their comfortable homes and move into a pioneering situation.

Physically it was not easy to start a settlement. The settlers had to live in tents and trailers, walk in mud, work hard, and suffer from a lack of water and electricity, but they were happy and knew that God was with them. Initially they were fortunate enough to have military generators to use for power, and military water tanks. People ask her if it was a difficult time, but Weiss says that it was like a continual festival without a moment of aggravation.

The Gush Emunim conducted a successful struggle against the Labor Government in those early years of developing Samaria and Binyamin. Daniella Weiss and her family, and Benny Katzover and his wife and three children, were among the first to live in an army camp just a little west of Shechem. They were happy to have a place to start their settlement even though their goal had been to live in ancient Shechem itself.

> Benny Katzover and Rav Menachem Felix formed a committee to attain the proper permits from the government for a settlement. Letters were sent to government members and ministers, including Prime Minister Golda Meir. They didn't ask for financial support. All they requested was a piece of land for a yeshiva (a religious school). The dream of the *garin* was to copy the example of Kiryat Arba by forming a Kiryat Shechem. They thought this would pave the way for the future settling of all of the Shomron and Binyamin.[3]

Here is the reason that the first Jewish settlement was not established in Samaria before 1975. When Benny and Felix were negotiating with Ariel Sharon and the Israeli government before the Yom Kippur War, Ariel Sharon had suggested that starting a settlement without government permission was something that

---

[3]Ibid, p. 4.

they should fast and pray about during Yom Kippur, and then meet again afterwards. But when the Yom Kippur War broke out, all this was delayed because all the men were called up for duty. At the end of the war, while the men were still in the army, the wives and women took it upon themselves to meet with Prime Minister Golda Meir about their goal to settle Samaria. She was surprised and shocked to hear what they wanted to do, but turned down any agreement for such an act.

Nonetheless the group continued pursuing its aim to establish the first Jewish settlement in Samaria – Kedumim – following the Yom Kippur War. The movement was known as "Garin Elon Moreh" and was led by Rabbi Menachem Felix, Benny Katzover, and Daniella Weiss. This was the same group that focused on renewing Jewish life in Samaria.

The name, Elon Moreh, is taken from the Bible in the book of Genesis:

> Abram traveled through the land as far as the site of the great tree of Moreh at Shechem.
>
> (Genesis 12:6)

Elon Moreh is another name for Shechem. Understanding the meaning of the choice of these two words, "Elon Moreh," will help one understand the background, life, purpose, and the goal of everything that was done in Samaria. This is not just the name of a place; it also incorporates the idea of returning to the heart of biblical history. It is full of symbols and deep meaning, including the return to the biblical city of Shechem where God first made a covenant with His people, the children of Israel, under the leadership of Joshua ben Nun in Samaria. Mount Gerizim and Mount Ebal are located in Samaria, and Joshua's altar can still be seen on Mount Ebal. This is the location and the place where all twelve tribes accepted the Torah, making Israel a nation. Now the Jews are waiting for the Messiah, who will make the Godly jump of establishing a nation that will once again be like it was under Joshua.

The Gush Emunim movement, which formed in 1974, came

mainly from one yeshiva in Jerusalem, called "Merkaz Harav." There were two major segments of Gush Emunim. One was called Garin Elon Moreh and the other developed in direct response to the Yom Kippur War.

> The spiritual leader and head of the yeshiva was Rabbi Zvi Yehuda Kook, the son of the revered Rabbi Avraham Isaac Kook, who had been in his day chief rabbi and one of the Jewish people's great spiritual leaders in the century.[4]

Rabbi Zvi Yehuda Kook was in his eighties when he inspired young people with the ideal of settling the areas of Judea and Samaria. In the 1970s, following the Yom Kippur War, these young people began to make plans for settling in Samaria. In 1974, Ariel Sharon, who was a member of Knesset (parliament of Israel), joined the young people who were trying to start the first settlement near the biblical town of Shechem. This was important for both national and security reasons. Rabbi Kook remained the leader until his death in 1982.

At first, Prime Minister Yitzhak Rabin was opposed to the idea just as Golda Meir had been. All the government people they spoke with felt that it would be wrong to move ahead without government permission, but in the end, the leaders of the Gush Emunim felt that they should push ahead with or without it. Finally, they decided to do this if they could get the blessing of Rabbi Zvi Yehuda Kook, who also felt that permission from the government would be better. With much trepidation they met with Rabbi Kook and brought up the subject. The Rav's response was:

> What do you want from me?

They answered that they wanted the Rav's blessing. He smiled, and with a warm handshake, blessed them that, God willing, they will be successful. They went home in high spirits.[5]

While they had Rabbi Kook's blessing there was still major

---

[4]*Warrior*, p. 362.
[5]*The Story of Benny Katzover*, p. 5.

opposition to the settlers for moving ahead without the government's permission. Some religious and government people wanted to keep focused on the Jordan Valley and the Golan Heights. But, at the same time, Shimon Peres, Minister of Transportation, was in favor of establishing settlements in the Shomron. In fact, he is quoted as saying, "Do the mountains of the Shomron fall short of the mountains of the Golan?"

Rabbi Kook requested a meeting with Peres to gain government support. Just before the meeting took place, Peres was given the position of Minister of Security in the Yitzhak Rabin government. When they did meet, Peres told Rabbi Kook that he did not have the authority to allow the settlers to settle in the Shomron. Then Rabbi Kook told Peres that if authority was not granted, he himself would join the settlers.

Both Rabbi Kook and Rabbi Chanan Porat served as the negotiators for the *garin* that was ready to settle in the Shomron (Samaria). Rabbi Porat had served as a paratrooper in the Six-Day War and was one of the liberators of the Temple Mount.[6] He was badly wounded in the Yom Kippur War of 1973, on the banks of the Suez Canal, but he recovered and was one of the founders of the Gush Emunim that eventually started more than 100 settlements.[7] In 1975, he led the founding of the first Jewish settlement in the Shomron near Sebastia.[8] The settlement was first known as Elon Moreh but now is Kedumim.

The people living in what is now Kedumim tried seven times to settle before the Israeli government finally allowed them to stay in Samaria, but not in Shechem as they wanted. These attempts included the location of the old train station of Sebastia that dates back to the Ottoman Empire. As explained previously, Sebastia was the former capital of Samaria during the time of King Omri of the northern kingdom.

---

[6]Keinon, Herb. *Happy Jerusalem Day*. Jerusalem Post. Retrieved 2008-12-15.

[7]Porat, Hanan. *nfc*. Retrieved 2008-12-15. (Hebrew)

[8]Gorenberg, Gershom. *Occupied Territories*. 2007, p. 316.

> In the thirty-first year of Asa king of Judah, Omri became king of Israel, and he reigned twelve years, six of them in Tirzah. He bought the hill of Samaria from Shemer for two talents of silver and built a city on the hill, calling it Samaria, after Shemer, the name of the former owner of the hill.
>
> (1 Kings 16:23-24)

The first seven attempts to start what is now the settlement of Kedumim were unsuccessful, because each time the government of Israel would come and force the settlers to leave after only a few days. The Israeli army would evacuate them, but this backfired on the government because every time the settlers were forced to leave, even more young people would come with food and building equipment for the next attempt to start the settlement.

It seems that the Jews are so strong that even the Jews themselves cannot stop the Jews who are Zionists and have the faith of Abraham, Isaac, and Jacob. So ... the thought of settling in Samaria began to take on a life of its own, and then continued to grow in popularity. Among the Jews there was a strong, earnest desire to reclaim their national heritage, which still has not died.

Ariel Sharon had the honor of driving Rabbi Kook to Samaria where his students were making the first of the seven attempts to start a settlement. Ariel Sharon drove Rabbi Kook to where his students were near Bad Shalosh, which today is an Israeli army base. Rabbi Kook joined in with those putting up tents, staking boundaries, and planting trees by planting a tree himself.

> All the while people were building and singing. There was no missing the spirit of it; the air was alive with the same kind of fellowship and determination that the kibbutzniks had had in earlier and harder times.[9]

In Ariel Sharon's biography, *Warrior*, he tells about how the army came to force the settlers to leave. An angry confrontation developed between the army and the settlers. The settlers

---

[9] *Warrior*, p. 263.

adamantly refused to go, and so Ariel used a military phone to contact Prime Minister Yitzhak Rabin about the situation. Although he negotiated with Sharon for a while, Rabin insisted that he could not allow the settlers to remain. Sharon was then able to offer a compromise to allow them to bed down in one of the nearby military bases in Samaria while waiting for a final decision.

However, even though Sharon was able to convince some of the young settlers that the compromise might eventually lead to the first successful settlement in Samaria, Rabbi Kook refused to embrace it. The young settlers said that when Rabbi Kook said "No" it truly meant no!

That evening a larger contingent of soldiers entered the compound and began dragging settlers away. The settlers passively resisted by holding onto rocks and dirt.

Sounds of scuffling and bodies scraping over the ground came from all over, and I saw a group of soldiers closing in on the Rabbi. The Rabbi was grasping a fence post determined not to leave. Sharon could not take this so he huddled himself over him to protect him.[10]

When the soldiers started pulling on Sharon, a large soldier then began to throw the soldiers out of the way and whispered to Sharon that he would not let anyone touch him. Rabbi Chanan Porat, who was also there supporting the settlers, was being forcefully pulled from the fence that he was hanging onto when Ariel Sharon said to the soldiers, "How dare you touch someone who was injured in the Yom Kippur War?"

Ariel Sharon felt such an identity with Rabbi Kook and the settlers that he left his car there and boarded the bus that the army had brought to transport the settlers away.[11]

After the settlers were removed, 30 families with their 50 children made a second attempt to establish a settlement on July 25, 1974. Once again this was in the location of the old Turkish train station near Sebastia. The core group was not alone

[10]Ibid, p. 363.

[11]*The Story of Benny Katzover*, p. 5.

because they were supported and joined by thousands of others, including rabbis, professors, authors, members of various youth movements, and Knesset members. For four days the masses continued to stream into the area via four prearranged routes.

Prime Minister Rabin was not happy with this settlement activity in Samaria and, after four days, he wanted the settlers removed again. Lt. General Mordechai "Motta" Gur, who was assigned to the Northern Front in 1974 following the Yom Kippur War toward the end of his long military career, debated with Rabin because he did not want to evacuate the settlers. He felt that it should be the job of the police, but Rabin ended up commanding the army to do it. Motta Gur arrived in Sebastia just after the Jewish holiday of Tisha B'Av (remembrance of the destruction of the first and second Temple). He negotiated with the leaders of the *garin* to have their people leave willingly, with the promise that he would find an alternative site for them. But the leaders turned him down in favor of a form of passive resistance known as "the potato sack." The evacuation started shortly after that and lasted five days. All this simply strengthened the support for settlements and the formation of even more *garinim*.

At the time that the settlers tried the third attempt to start a settlement in Samaria, settlers of other *garinim* were attempting to start settlements including Shiloh, Jericho, and Elkana. The new strategy was to have so many settlements in so many different locations at the same time that evacuation by the government would be more complicated and costly. They hoped that this would mean that the settlers would have more time for establishing each settlement.

On October 22, 1974, thousands gave up the celebration of Simchat Torah to be a part of the third attempt to start Kedumim. Because Shimon Peres was criticized so much for not preventing the previous attempts, he had roadblocks set up on all the major roads in anticipation of another attempt to establish settlements in Samaria. Because of the roadblocks, the *garinim* and the Gush Emunim had the people split up into 16 smaller groups. The next day the headlines in the newspapers said that Rabbi Yochanan

Freed, Gush Emunim spokesman, had established 16 settlements in the Shomron and Binyamin (parts of Samaria). The press got the impression that all of these groups had started settlements that quickly. Since thousands of people were so scattered, it took a whole week for the government to locate and evacuate all the settlers. This worked more in favor of the settlers than they expected. Their purpose in having so many small groups was that it would distract from the Garin Elon Moreh. This resulted in the Gush Emunim movement being taken much more seriously.

About March 22, 1975, the settlers of Garin Elon Moreh made a fourth unsuccessful attempt to start a settlement near Sebastia. Following that, both their fifth and sixth attempts also ended with ugly clashes between the settlers and the Israeli army. A march to promote interest in a settlement in the Shomron then took place during Passover week of 1975, when 20,000 people marched from the Moshav Shaar Efraim, which is just east of Netanya near the Green Line, all the way to the Sebastia train station. The settlement of Ofra was started in the Spring of 1975, when settlers built a fence around an old Jordanian army base followed by settlers moving onto the army base.

There was some discussion about the possibility of the people who were part of Garin Elon Moreh giving up their idea of starting a settlement in Samaria and joining the Ofra settlement, but most of them decided to keep on with the struggle. On July 22, 1975, the date of the sixth attempt to establish Kedumim (Garin Elon Moreh), the would-be settlers tried to copy what the people of Garin Ofra had done. They organized themselves into a civilian work crew for the department of defense and commuted from Tel Aviv every day for two weeks before spending the night in the Sebastia train station. They thought perhaps this would fool the government administration. However, after two nights, the government realized what their motive was and forced them to evacuate.

In order to keep the connection alive, the settlers then found reasons to visit and hold special events, such as weddings at the ancient Sebastia train station. When it appeared that there might not be another attempt to start Kedumim because support was waning, Benny Katzover and Menachem Felix threatened to leave Gush Emunim, but in the end they stayed when the Gush Emunim people as a whole decided on a seventh attempt, just a week before Hanukkah. This time the plan was to try in a more quiet and peaceful way, but if that failed then they planned to involve thousands of people once more. Again the soldiers came and began to move them out. At this point, Menachem Felix said, "It's true that we're knocking our heads against the wall. But our heads are harder than the wall, and eventually the wall will collapse."

Daniella Weiss describes how the seven attempts eventually led to success on the eighth attempt, and that this matches what the Bible tells us in Proverbs 24:16: "For though a righteous man falls seven times, he rises again."

> On the third night of Hanukkah in 1975, tens of thousands marched in the rain and cold to Sebastia, the ancient train station. The rain did not dampen the spirits of those who had come to celebrate Hanukkah in support of establishing the first settlement in Samaria. Like the Maccabees of old, these pioneering founders were determined to embrace their heritage while strengthening the presence of the Jewish people in Samaria.

Some reported that it seemed like suddenly the whole valley was lit up because of the thousands of marchers each holding their candles. A newspaper in Israel ran a political cartoon, using four of the Hanukkah candles to show how the four leaders of the Garin Elon Moreh who started Kedumim were illuminated in the light of the candles, which is God's light, while the rest of Israel in the cartoon were enjoying their comfortable lives in the cities, but remained in darkness. This cartoon was in support of those who had braved the odds seven times to finally succeed on the eighth attempt to start a Jewish community in Samaria. It was a bit surprising since it ran in a national newspaper not favorably disposed to the settlers. The caption under the cartoon read "The light of Elon Moreh." This was not something that the settlers had put in the newspapers, but the cartoon was drawn by a person in Israel who was not a settler or for the settlements, but who had great respect for the stamina of the settlers. This showed that more and more Jews in Israel were supporting the settlements.

Even though Yitzhak Rabin tried to stop what was happening, the settlers managed to stay for eight days. During that time friends smuggled in food and building materials via various roads, and a few structures were established. Many leaders also came to the train station to show solidarity by attending the dedication of the school, kindergarten, post office, and a medical clinic.

At that point, Prime Minister Rabin called for a special meeting of his ministers to discuss the situation. Most of them favored the evacuation of the settlement. However, when the Prime Minister, Commander Motta Gur, and Shimon Peres flew over the settlement in a helicopter and saw the adults and the children who were on the ground, they became concerned that a forced evacuation might cause injuries. Peres was chosen to visit the settlement to try to present a compromise. When he arrived he was met with singing and dancing, but the joy was short lived because he announced that the settlement would have to be evacuated.

*Some of Samaria's first settlers.*

The settlers were outraged. Chaim Guri, a poet and journalist, then suggested a compromise. Rather than evacuating the settlers from the Shomron as they had done before, he suggested that the government allow them to stay in an old army camp not too far from Sebastia. With Ariel Sharon's help, a vote of the *garin* leadership resulted in their accepting the compromise, even though Rav Levinger was opposed. In the end, an agreement was written up by Peres to allow 30 settlers, out of the hundreds of supporters, to live on the military base.

At the beginning of their stay, the settlers worked for the military, but it was not guaranteed that the settlers would be allowed to stay permanently. Thus the government was in shock when the news portrayed the agreement as a victory for the settlers and not for the government.

Eventually, in 1975, on their eighth attempt, the settlers of the Garin Elon Moreh group were allowed to settle permanently in what is today Kedumim, taking up residence in an old army base called Kadum, located eleven kilometers west of Shechem and Sebastia. Thirty families began to live in an abandoned prison area of the former army camp, under horrific conditions without adequate water or electricity. They used a communal kitchen and a one-room concrete army barracks, plus tents for housing in the middle of winter. Indications are that these were very tough and determined people.

The Israeli government under Yitzhak Rabin, who was then in his first term, prevented the first attempts by settlers to settle in Samaria, arguing that their main aim was to secure permanent Israeli possession of Samaria, and that such possession would preclude any possibility of peace with Jordan or a Palestinian state. His concerns were right because that was exactly what the settlers wanted. They believe that the mountains of Israel belong to the Jews and their goal was to establish many Jewish communities in Samaria.

Even after the government gained control of Samaria from Jordan during the Six-Day War, they were ready to give it up again if doing so would mean permanent peace. Defense

Minister Shimon Peres was the person who first authorized both the settlements of Kedumim in Samaria and Ofra in Binyamin. However, he was accused of helping the settlers as part of his ongoing power struggle with Rabin. Yitzhak Rabin was not willing to counter Peres's decision. After Shimon Peres granted permission for the settlers to stay, Prime Minister Rabin agreed. God even uses politics to accomplish his purposes.

Rabin's approval was a tactical one. He believed that the attention surrounding the evacuations had had the effect of strengthening the settlers.

> Let's allow them to move in to Camp Kadum (now Kedumim), he said. Within three weeks they'll leave on their own.[12]

Instead of getting tired and leaving, now 600,000 Jews are now living in Judea and Samaria when you include the population of East Jerusalem, which is also technically called disputed land by some.

Immediately following the agreement, cars began streaming to the army base where families and singles would live in army tents and shacks for four months until they shifted to a community of mobile homes on top of a nearby hill, to form the first settlement in Samaria. In 1977, right after Menachem Begin of the Likud Party won the election and became the new prime minister, he made an official visit to Kedumim.

Shimon Peres must be given credit for helping establish the roots of the settler movement in Samaria. On the other hand, some of the left-wing politicians equated this with the "original sin" of Adam and Eve. Also the Labor government held onto the deed to Kadum, which was the name of the army base to show that the government was in charge. Peres allowed the settlers to put down their roots and start the growth of the settlement movement.

In Ariel Sharon's autobiography, *Warrior*, he describes some of the issues regarding the land of Samaria following the Six-Day

---

[12]Ibid, p. 9.

War and the Yom Kippur War. He played a part in the planning and decisions while serving as Minister of Agriculture. Sharon had been thinking about the need for having Jewish settlements in Samaria right after the Six-Day War, which is why he started military training schools in all the former Jordanian army camps. His hope was that the former military bases would eventually become Jewish communities. He knew this is the very thing that happened in the Jordan Valley before the Yom Kippur War.

Sharon loved Samaria and did all he could to research the land to enjoy the land of the Bible. He walked the area several times while serving as an advisor to Menachem Begin and tells about how it was climbing the hills and walking over fields of rocks.

In 1974, and 1975, the settlement movement accelerated. A big factor was the change in the Israeli government from the Labor Party's view of Israel and Samaria to that of the right-wing view under the Likud Party. There were politicians who leaned toward the left in their political views, who wrote after the Six-Day War that the Jews should return right away to Judea and Samaria, stressing the urgency of moving the Jews into the areas taken so that Israel would not return again to its previous situation that kept its citizens from visiting or living in Samaria. Before there were settlements in the mountains, Israel's enemies threatened the Israelis from a geographically high, advantageous position.

The Labor Party wanted to keep Jews out of Samaria because they believed they might want to use the land of Samaria as a bargaining chip for peace with Jordan. They considered giving the control over Samaria back to Jordan, but it was Shimon Peres, the defense minister, who gave permission for Ofra as well as Kedumim to be established.

Yitzhak Rabin made a compromise with the settlers when he defeated Shimon Peres for leadership of the Labor Party and became the prime minister of Israel in 1974. He succeeded Golda Meir after she resigned and served as prime minister until the Likud Party defeated the Labor Party in 1977, with Menachem

*A prayer service on a barren hilltop held by some of Samaria's first settlers.*

Begin assuming the office of prime minister. The Labor Party controlled the government from 1948 through 1975, when settlers were trying to start settlements in Samaria. At first Rabin was part of the struggle against the settlers, but later he was on the side of the settlers.

Daniella Weiss, who was the mayor of Kedumim for 15 years, tells about those early days in the army camp and setting up the first housing. She came to Kedumim 35 years ago, with her husband and her two daughters, Yael and Sheila. At that time the beautiful hill where Kedumim is today was just a bare hill. They started in tents, moved from there to shacks, then to trailers, then to a little better housing, and now 40 years later, they live in a very nice home. What makes her the happiest now is that her daughters and grandchildren are part of the settlements and the team of Jews reclaiming the Land. She is so thrilled that she has spent the last 40 years focusing on building communities in the Shomron.

She has prayed every Shabbat that her children and the young people she teaches would follow in her footsteps, and now she can see the fruit of her influence. She remembers so vividly when her daughter, Sheila, and her husband, Shivi, came into her living room and announced that they wanted to start a new community. Daniella's husband asked why when things were so comfortable in Kedumim. The other daughter said to her father that her sister Sheila and her husband and their six children were simply following in the footsteps of her grandparents and parents. The grandparents left the comforts of their home country of Hungary to come to Israel, and following their example, her parents left the comforts of their Tel Aviv home to pioneer the first settlement in the barren Shomron. Daniella's daughter, Yael, went on to say that they and all of those who are following her are also following in the footsteps of Abraham, Isaac, and Jacob.[13]

Another one of the original group of Kedumim settlers was Shoshana Shilo, who explains that even though she felt that they were opening Samaria for the Jewish people, they did not really know the price that they would pay for settling in Samaria. As explained before, that price included not having water or electricity, not having suitable housing for a long time, and also the suffering caused by what they called the Oslo war. Her father, who came to Israel 70 years earlier and helped establish the first religious kibbutz in Israel, taught her that whatever the cost, their effort was not for them, but for future generations. With this in mind they persevered, even though hundreds of Jews in Judea and Samaria were murdered during the intifada. Shoshana also says that God is in control and is with the Jewish people, and because He will never leave them, they will never leave the Land until they see the redemption.

## The Late Ron Nachman, Blessed Be His Memory, and Ariel

As mentioned in an earlier chapter, the settlement Ariel in Samaria eventually became the city, Ariel. It was no accident that Ariel also became the largest city in Samaria with a population of 20,000. It is also the home of Ariel University. The leaders of the settlement movement felt the need for a larger settlement that

---

[13]Ridgley, Ezra B, *The Spring of Judea and Samaria*, Video, 2012.

*Ron Nachman.*

would provide services for the smaller settlements in the area.

Ron Nachman was the chairman of Garin Tel Aviv, the organized group that started the settlement of Ariel. He remembers how Defense Minister Moshe Dayan called on young people to help with the defense of the country and the settlement movement. Ron and others responded in a letter to Moshe, telling him that they were forming a group that would start a settlement. Moshe answered with the encouraging news that he would help them with their plans by encouraging the government to allocate some land to them. The group and the plans were underway before the Yom Kippur War, but that put everything on hold for four years. Many in the *garin* were then called up to fight in the war. After the war they chose to use the principles used by the early Kibbutz movement for establishing Ariel. They used questionnaires, interviews, home visits, and monthly membership dues, to determine who would be part of the initial group. Nearly 6,000 people joined and competed for a place in it.

Ron was very disappointed that, due to a change in Israeli politics, the settlement movement now had less support. Yet the settlement movement, according to Ben Gurion, was a key element in the development of a Jewish homeland.

> Since Oslo, however, the idea of settlement has been denigrated and belittled. Let me make this clear: without settlements, there would be no Israel. Moreover, the Left began accusing us of being "occupiers," but if this is our land, if we have the right to this land – and we do – then we are not occupiers, but we are the rightful owners of the Land.[14]

Ariel started in 1978 with 40 pioneering families who came, not only to live in very primitive conditions, but were willing to move stones on a rocky, barren hill and start developing the Land. They understood the importance of establishing a Jewish presence in such a strategic area.

Mayor Ron Nachman said:

> I cannot but remember the bare, rocky hilltop we chose to call home. Our home was a mountain that had no name, but the name our Arab neighbors chose to call it, "Hill of Death." They called it that because they believed they believed that nothing could ever flourish on that hill.[15]

The Ariel pioneers arrived in 1978 with two tents and a mutual dream. Ron was one of those who dreamed of a modern city. As elsewhere there were no viable roads, no running water, and no electricity, but they came in faith, determined to turn the barren mountain into a flourishing community. Even though the Arabs thought they were crazy, they were not opposed to the

[14]Nachman, Ron. Interview. A publication of the aliyah and absorption committee of the city of Ariel, *Shalom Ariel*, 2008.
[15]Ibid.

idea. In fact, those early Jewish pioneers did their shopping in the nearby Arab town of Salfit.

During the first ten years those living in tents moved into mobile homes and the mobile home areas grew into new neighborhoods. The population grew to 2,000 with 70 school-aged children, which led to the building of the first school. Industry sprang up where there had been only sagebrush that provided employment for the residents. Those who met the criteria to start Ariel included doctors, nurses, teachers, and business people who were a great asset to the initial community.

The medical needs in Ariel were first met by a medical health clinic that opened in 1978 with one nurse, Jana Schultz, working out of one room. At first Jana treated people with her own first aid supplies.

> In those "primitive" times, before electricity and sidewalks, Jana recalls being called to many patients in the middle of the night. On one rainy evening she received a call for help. (There was no phones then!) Jana pulled on her husband's galoshes, and ran to assist. She arrived, to assist. However, she arrived with only one boot as the other one had been sucked off her foot by the squelching mud![16]

After a few weeks a doctor from another settlement began coming to Ariel twice a week, in the evenings, to treat people by candlelight if the generator was not working. Now people look back with nostalgia, remembering how they often stood outside the small clinic in the pouring winter rain to wait while someone else was inside being treated. In 1982, medical services were much improved and offered by the National Health Service, so that the 200 residents finally had a choice of doctors and facilities.

Here I want to include one personal account from the early settlers in Samaria.

> My husband Yaakov and I immigrated to Israel from the former Soviet Union in January 1972. We were ardent

---

[16]*Shalom Ariel*, Autumn, 2008.

Zionists and we had to fight the Soviet establishment in order to obtain immigration permits to come to Israel. We vowed we would find a way to contribute to the building and growing of Israel, just like the Jews of the first Aliyah.

We heard about Ariel and in the summer of 1978, after going through testing and being accepted, we found ourselves on a rocky hill with another 30 families. We did not know anyone.

One evening, I sent my son to borrow a cup of flour from one of our neighbors. Five minutes later, he was back crying bitterly and covered in blood from a fall.

There was no doctor or clinic in Ariel and I did not know what to do or where to turn. A neighbor heard us and ran to bring a nurse. The nurse cleaned the wound and told us to take our son to the hospital because he needed stitches. The neighbors quickly organized in less than thirty minutes a car for us with an armed driver. (In those days, the road to Ariel was unpaved and wound through every Arab village.)

This was our first encounter with the first families that settled Ariel. I knew that these were the kind of people I wanted as neighbors. We came to Ariel because of ideology, but we stayed because of the people.[17]

Mayor Ron Nachman passed away after a long fight with cancer in January of 2013.

## Elon Moreh

Three years after the successful establishment of Kedumim, in 1978, Rabbi Menachem Felix and Benny Katzover brought together 17 of the 80 families living in Kedumim to begin a settlement closer to Shechem. The Jews know how important Shechem is in Jewish history because it is where Abraham traveled, where Jacob purchased land, and where Joseph is buried. The settlers were encouraged to try once again to settle in Shechem or close to it, because they felt that Prime Minister

---

[17]Feitelson, Leah. *Shalom Ariel*, Autumn, 2008.

Menachem Begin was on their side in the struggle to reclaim and settle Samaria. But even with a right-wing government supporting them, it was a struggle to start another settlement.

It turned out that even Begin was opposed to a Jewish settlement in the town of Shechem (Nablus) because of feared problems from the Arabs. Regarding this, the settlers struggled against Begin and the government policy for two years. Because of their strong desire for a settlement in Shechem, the Jews of the Garin Elon Moreh Two were finally allowed to set up mobile homes in an area known today as Itamar, but known then as Rajeb. It was near the Itamar of today that was started six years later in 1984 by a different nucleus or *garin* of settlers. In August 1978, the same day of the signing of the Camp David Accords, the Garin Elon Moreh Two settled a hilltop southwest of Shechem called Rujib.

By 1978, the Elon Moreh settlement number two at Rujib faced a big problem because the Arabs in the area complained to the supreme court about their land being taken over by Jews. This resulted in the government ordering this settlement to be dismantled by the end of 1979. Fortunately for the settlers, an Israel army commander of the area named Luntz very enthusiastically supported the Jewish desire for the settlement of Garin Elon Moreh Two. He wanted to help them move from Rujib, the first location of Elon Moreh Two, which had been declared Arab land, to another area. When the court told the settlers that they had only one month to evacuate the settlement, Commander Luntz did everything in his power to find a new location for the settlement.

He offered the settlers an area that was state land and for sure not Arab land. This meant that the local Arabs would not be able to dispute the ownership of that land. Commander Luntz encouraged them to move to what is today the settlement of Elon Moreh and even helped the settlers by building roads for them. This commander was loved very much by the Jewish settlers. In 1980, Prime Minister Rabin approved the site suggested by Commander Luntz and the settlers  moved to state land offered by Commander Luntz as an authorized settlement, Elon Moreh, which is located today at the base of Mount Kabir. After the first settlement in Samaria was named Kedumim, after the name of the army base where it started, the Garin Elon Moreh decided to apply the name "Elon Moreh" to the second settlement to be started in the vicinity of Shechem. This is how the settlement near Mount Kabir received its name.

There has always been a debate concerning state land and private land in Samaria and Judea. As mentioned before, state land is land that was originally owned by the Ottoman Empire, which was passed on to the British before being placed in the hands of Jordan after the 1948 War of Independence. Israel gained control of this same land by defeating Jordan during the Six-Day War. Private land is land owned or used by private individuals. Israel has tried to avoid taking control of private land owned by Arabs when approving the start of new Jewish settlements.

The growth of current settlements and the addition of more new settlements continue to this day. Following the establishment of Elon Moreh, Elkana and Ma'ale Adumim were started. More and more settlements were started with help from Ariel Sharon, including Beit El, Shilo, Karnei Shomron, and Ariel. In 1979, the first regional office for Samaria was opened. In 1984, the settlement known today as Itamar was started near the first location of the settlers of Garin Elon Moreh Two.

## Moshe Zar

Another pioneering hero is Moshe Zar (Czar), whose family made aliyah to Israel from Iran before he was born. Even so he came into the world in Jerusalem in 1938, before Israel was recognized as an independent country. Currently he is married with eight children.

During their first years of marriage, he and his family lived in Moshav Nehalim near Petah Tikva, west of Ariel. Thirty years ago, in 1981, his children began to ask him why they just talked about the need for people to settle in Samaria, but did not move there. That same year they did move to the Karnei Shomron settlement where he supported himself as an electrical contractor.

The hilltop on which he now lives is near Karnei Shomron and is called Mitzpe Tzvaim, which means "the place to view a deer." He built his house by himself with help

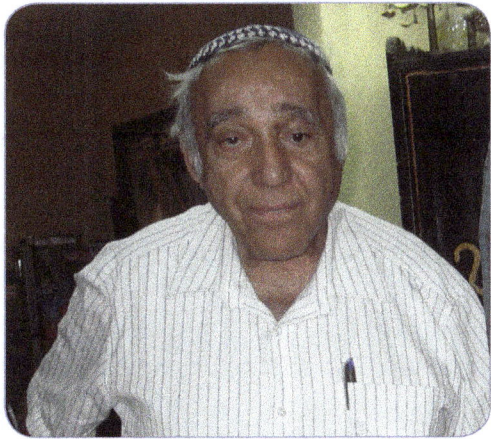

*Moshe Zar.*

from his sons on a hilltop that he purchased from the Arabs, and he has the paper to prove the transaction. He bought the land, designed, and built a large house because of his large family, and because he wanted a strong house that would not be easy for the Israeli government to come and dismantle. He has successfully lived in this house since 1981.

Moshe Zar's children are all now grown and married and they all live in various settlements in Judea and Samaria. He and his wife enjoy their many grandchildren and great-grandchildren. His descendants are spread out all over Judea and Samaria in places like Mitzpe Yericho, which is near ancient Jericho, and Har Bracha on Mount Gerizim.

Tragically, the Palestinians murdered Moshe's son, Gilad. Losing his son, who was such a help to him, hurt him very deeply. Gilad lived in the Itamar settlement that he helped build before he was murdered by Palestinian terrorists on May 29, 2001, while driving from the settlement of Kedumim to the settlement of Yitzhar. His wife, Hagar, and eight children survive Gilad. Since he was murdered, four of his daughters have married and two of them now live in Itamar. Moshe has the good fortune to have all his children and grandchildren following in his footsteps by living in the biblical heartland.

The most interesting aspect of Moshe's story involves his

well-known ability to purchase Arab land. This was not initially a problem because the Arabs wanted to sell their land because they needed the money and there was a pleasant working relationship between the Jews and the Arabs. For example, when he got involved in negotiations with Arabs in the beginning, he did not need to carry any weapons with him. There could be problems, but overall the whole situation was more peaceful than it is today. He registered the land that he has purchased under his own name so that there would be more places besides state land for Jews to live in Samaria and Judea legally.

Moshe bought a lot of land as a result of his mixing with the Arab people and asking those who worked for him about land that he might buy. His good relationship with the Arabs enabled him to go to the head of each Arab village to discuss the land he wanted to purchase, to be absolutely sure whom the land belonged to. He would never buy land if he did not know who legally owned it.

At the same time, when the word got out that he had the money to buy land and was willing to pay a good price for it, many Arabs who wanted to sell would come to him to work out a fair price. He was able to discuss the details and agree on a purchase price that the Arabs were happy with. And, he was careful to be sure that he bought each piece of land via a legal transaction with the proper paperwork, including an official notarization stamp. In no way could anyone ever say that he was stealing land from the Arabs.

However, now the problem with using any land legally purchased originates not entirely with the Arabs, but with the Israeli government, which is afraid to recognize Moshe's purchases. Moshe says that he has to present the documentation to the government as if he were in court trying to prove a legal case. It has been very difficult for him to get the government to accept his legal documentation. The government officials continue to refuse to accept it and will not register the land he has purchased under his name, as a private party from private individuals. It seems that there is so much stigma and false reports about Jews taking land away from the Arabs illegally that the Israeli government is afraid to recognize that Moshe's transactions are completely legal. No matter how hard Moshe Zar worked in order to make Jewish settlements on private land legal, it seems that the Israeli government wants to avoid anything that could possibly smell like trouble with the United States or Europe.

Unfortunately, due to the intifada and the leadership of Yasser Arafat, relationships between the Arabs and the Jews greatly deteriorated. As a result, Arab land can no longer be purchased easily, because the Palestinian leadership threatens to kill any Arab landowner who sells land to a Jew. At the same time, land that has already been bought and paid for is waiting for settlers to develop it, if only the Israeli government would recognize earlier purchases. There is plenty of land in Samaria; indeed, the land already purchased could easily support forty or fifty thousand more residents according to Moshe Zar. So far only five settlements have been started on the land that Moshe has purchased. In most countries anyone, whether a citizen or not, can buy property if they have the money to do so. So we must ask why this should not be the case in Samaria.

Moshe's reaction to the tragic killing of his son, Gilad Zar, is to build six new communities, one for each of the six Hebrew letters that make up the Hebrew name "Gilad Zar." This will serve as a memorial to the body and soul of his son, who worked hard to develop and expand the settlements. Starting these new settlements brings comfort to Moshe who was so hurt by the loss of his son. So far four of the six have been started on property that Moshe himself has purchased.

The settlement closest to his home is called Ramat Gilad, and another near Kedumim is Havat Gilad. He is not willing to say where the other two small settlements are, which he started recently. He will not give their names or locations because he does not want to draw the Israeli government's attention. He is trying to protect these settlements from both the Israeli government and international pressure groups. The problem is further amplified by groups like Peace Now, who are deliberately stirring up the Arabs against the Jews.

In the case of Ramat Gilad, the government is requiring that some of the homes be moved to a location closer to the larger settlement of Karnei Shomron, because they are said to be on private land belonging to the Arabs. There really should not be any issue because it is private land that was legally purchased by Moshe Zar.

Moshe has always lived on good terms with Arabs who want to live in peace. He does feel that the Israeli government needs to expel Arabs who insist on causing trouble and unrest. He says that no citizen should be allowed to throw rocks at police or private citizens, use guns, or bombs of any kind. He and other Jews desire a good relationship with Arabs, but tough law enforcement with proper punishment is the language that the Arabs understand. He said that if the Arabs were to rule in Samaria then the Jews would not be able to live here. Jews who do try to live where the Arabs rule are treated very poorly. For example Jews were killed in Hebron and Shechem and their dead bodies were dragged with vehicles in order to show as much disrespect and hatred for the Jews as possible.

Moshe told me that there are many Jews who want to leave the well-established parts of Israel and move to Judea and Samaria, which means there is a need for more land to be purchased and developed. According to Moshe there are about 500,000 people living in Judea and Samaria right now, and such a large number of people should make the Israeli government take all this very seriously.

Israel needs to realize that the growth and development of the settlements and communities in Israel will continue in spite of the hindrances caused by both the left-wing Jews and the radical Arabs. Any time a house in Samaria is dismantled or destroyed by the Israeli government, many more will be built in place of the one destroyed, according to Moshe. This will go on forever, with houses torn down and rebuilt and torn down and rebuilt over and over and over, because the Jews will never give up living in the heartland of Israel.

I have already quoted Ariel Sharon earlier in this book. Ariel Sharon was a champion of the settlement movement, but tragically things changed. He was Moshe Zar's commander during the Yom Kippur War, and as a result they were close friends for many years. Moshe told me that at least once a week Sharon would come to his home and sit with him on the roof over a meal or a cup of coffee and discuss how they could get more Jews to settle in Samaria. Sharon would say to him:

> Come on, let's build more settlements and let's get more Jews to come and live out here.

Then, according to Moshe, there was a major change in Ariel Sharon that caused him to take the action that he did against Gush Katif and other communities in the disengagement of Gaza. He said that Ariel Sharon is no longer his friend because there was no reason at all for destroying communities in Gaza. Sharon removed 8,000 Jews who had developed one of the best agriculture projects in the world. Even as I write this, as a result of the expulsion from Gaza many of those people still do not have a permanent place to live. Moshe compares what happened to Sharon to a barrel of cream that someone adds a cup of poison to. "Is the cream still cream? No, the cream has now become poison. What Sharon did in the latter part of his life overshadowed all the good things that he did before."[18]

Moshe told me that he really appreciates it when people who are not Jewish understand the situation in Samaria. These are people who understand what the Bible says about the land and its people. And, of course, he wishes that Jews who are in exile all over the world would pack up their things and come back to the land to settle here in Samaria and Judea, so that many new settlements can be established. He said that, in his opinion, anyone is welcome to come and live in this area, if they are willing to live in peace as law-abiding citizens who want to live together peacefully with the Jews. This could include Muslims,

---

[18]From author's interview.

Christians, or anyone. For example even if an Egyptian wants to come and buy some property and live here in peace, that is fine. But if they come to fight against the other citizens and not live peacefully, then they should be required to leave. To Moshe it is a black-and-white situation with no gray in the middle.

Moshe Zar is a wonderful, humble man and a legend because of his ability to purchase land and because of his part in encouraging Jews to settle in Samaria. Pioneers like Moshe Zar should be recognized as much as those famous Jews who started the settlements that led to a Jewish nation.

> Moshe Zar is a Zionist. He was a soldier in the 1956 war when he was wounded very seriously. He purchased a lot of land in Samaria from the Arabs, including where the settlement of Imanu'el is located. It was his example that led other Jews to buy land for the establishment of more communities. It is hard to describe how much land was purchased and communities started as a result of his land purchases, but then the Israeli government took a lot of that land and gave it back to the Arabs. During his time in Samaria he was attacked and seriously wounded by an Arab. Terrorists killed his son Gilad who was quite famous. He has grandchildren who are activists in the settlement movement. He was a friend of Ariel Sharon in the army. He was a paratrooper and was injured near the Suez Canal during the battle of Mitla, a narrow passage in the mountains, during the Yom Kippur War where many lost their lives.[19]

## Professor Hillel Weiss

Another pioneering settler that I interviewed for this book is Professor Hillel Weiss, who was born in Israel in 1945. His father migrated to Israel from Budapest, Hungary, while his mother came from the Belarus area of Lithuania. Hillel was a paratrooper in the Six-Day War. He has six grandchildren who currently live in Hebron. He is a respected professor at Bar Ilan University and a leader who has been an advocate for settlements and lives

---

[19]From author's interview.

in a settlement. He has been a spokesman for the need for settlements as far back as 1972 before the Yom Kippur War. In 1977, he and his wife and five children were among the founders of the settlement of Elkana located just east of the Green Line.

Just a year and a half after the start of Kedumim, the government gave permission to start the settlement of Elkana.

*Hillel Weiss.*

Hillel and his family, with others started out living in mobile homes in some very tough circumstances, but have seen the their efforts develop over the years into a settlement of 800 families and a population of about 4,000, with beautiful permanent homes and paved streets. For the first seven years his family lived in a small mobile home, willing to sacrifice the comforts of a large home in order to put their feet where their heart was. It was crowded for a family of five children that increased to seven while living in the settlement, but they were so happy living where God wanted them.

Eventually Professor Weiss's parents moved to Elkana, and when his mother passed away she was the first person to be buried in Elkana. Hillel had a struggle trying to convince the other settlers that his mother needed to be buried in the settlement, but he was very adamant about her being buried there and nowhere else. The people thought that if they were forced by the government to leave Elkana and if Jews were buried there, the Arabs would come and dig up the bodies. They could not bear thinking about that. But Professor Weiss finally convinced them and since then there have been at least 100 people buried in Elkana. The burial of Jews in a settlement means that it is less likely to given up.

At the time of this interview Professor Weiss told me that there were 600,000 Jewish settlers over the Green Line in Judea and Samaria, including about 100,000 settlers near Jerusalem. The Israeli government could have annexed Judea and Samaria legally like they annexed East Jerusalem, the Golan Heights, and other territories in 1948 and 1949 (although Jordan still laid claim to the West Bank until 1988).

Because Israel gained control of Judea and Samaria while defending itself, and because of the law passed by the League of Nations in 1920, setting aside the land for a Jewish homeland, the West Bank area could have been annexed by Israel. Many countries did not recognize Jordan's annexation of Judea and Samaria. In 1920, after WWI, the League of Nations voted to sign the San Remo document so that Israel could have a home country that would include the West Bank and the Trans-Jordan.

The British were given the task by the League of Nations and the UN to bring Palestine to where the Jews could handle it as an independent nation.

In 1922, Britain decided against part of the law that gave the Jews both the West Bank and the Trans-Jordan as voted by the League of Nations, by giving the Trans-Jordan to King Abdullah. But they did confirm that all of the West Bank would be the home of the Jews.

In 1925, Calvin Coolidge, president of the United States, signed into law the stipulation that all the land west of the Jordan would be a homeland for the Jews, all the way from the Jordan River to the Mediterranean Sea. Coolidge expressed his "sympathy with the deep and intense longing which finds such fine expression in the Jewish National Homeland in Palestine."[20]

The American Congress was no less sympathetic to the Zionist objective. One can look back to the joint congressional resolutions of 1922 and 1944 that unanimously passed separate endorsements of the Balfour Declaration. In 1922, the House Foreign Affairs Committee also stated:

---

[20]*Roots of the U.S.-Israel Relationship,* www.jewishvirtuallibrary.org

The Jews of America are profoundly interested in establishing a National Home in the ancient land for their race. Indeed, this is the ideal of the Jewish people, everywhere, for, despite their dispersion, Palestine has been the object of their veneration since they were expelled by the Romans. For generations they have prayed for the return to Zion. During the past century this prayer has assumed practical form.

Legislatures in 33 states, representing 85 percent of the population, also adopted resolutions favoring the creation of a Jewish state in Palestine. Governors of 37 states, 54 United States senators, and 250 congressmen signed petitions to the President.[21]

Herbert Hoover, the 31st president of the United States, also supported Zionism.

Palestine, desolate for centuries, is now renewing its youth and vitality through enthusiasm, hard work, and self-sacrifice of the Jewish pioneers who toil there in a spirit of peace and social justice.[22]

According to Professor Hillel Weiss, the United Nations is now acting against the laws that were passed in favor of a Jewish homeland, even though such laws are still on the books. Weiss also said that the Jews are under the illusion that the Arabs will get on their knees and ask the Jews if they really want the land or not. So, part of the problem is the Jewish people themselves. It was a French Catholic Priest and not a Jew who said that, after 1967, the Jews should build the third Temple and reinstitute the sacrificial system. Hillel Weiss also said that non-Jews expect the Jews to be Jews, but it is the Jews who are reticent to be Jews and seem to be happy to be assimilated. Thus some of the Jews seem to be denying their own identity. They say that they are not Jews, but Israelis. Their willingness to sell the West Bank and the Sinai amounts to giving up their rights.

---

[21] Ibid.

[22] Ibid.

Hillel Weiss told me that individual Arabs did not make a claim for the bulk of the land. Most of the Jews in Samaria are strong about their identity, but the State still seems to become like the God of the Jewish people. Hillel said that the Jews say, "God has given the Jews a State after 2,000 years so now we cannot speak against the State." Some rabbis are saying that the State of Israel is the throne of God, and the soldiers are serving the throne of God, so who can then speak against the State? So Hillel and others are organizing "to cure the Jewish people from all of these stupid ideas. We are making a covenant regarding all of these topics."

A year ago, when the movement started, one of the goals was for Jews to know their legal rights in the Land. Not only their rights as based on the Bible, but also based on what the League of Nations signed, to the effect that the Land of Israel is to be a homeland for the Jewish people. But the nations have forgotten about it and most of the Jewish people did not want to hear about it.

> In 1922, the idea of a Jewish homeland received formal, international support when the League of Nations approved the British Mandate of Palestine, entrusting Great Britain with establishing a homeland for the Jewish people in Palestine. The Balfour Declaration, legislated five years earlier by the British Parliament, was the first time a world power recognized the need for a homeland for the Jewish people; now, that need has achieved international recognition.[23]

Yoel Lerner, linguist, translator, and educator, wrote a letter to UN Secretary-General Ban Ki-moon warning him that going against what the League of Nations passed in 1922 is wrong, and that by his claiming that Palestine belongs to the Palestinians he is speaking maliciously against the Jews. In the same letter Lerner presented a lawsuit against 26 European leaders who claim that

---

[23]History of Israel, League of Nations: Creating a Mandate State. Website: Stand with Israel.

the land, especially the West Bank, belongs to the Palestinians and not the Jews. The letter was signed by four mayors of municipalities in the Yesha and was delivered by the Director of the Foreign Affairs. Bibi Netanyahu stated in the United States that the Jews are not conquerors in their own land.

Professor Hillel Weiss said that there has been talk of plans for a railroad to be constructed from Tel Aviv to Ariel, with eventual connections with Syria and Jordan. According to the plan there would be a line from Eilat to Syria with additional lines to Jordan. According to him there are UN discussions about the construction of such. This has been mapped out and a feasibility study has been done. Many of the mayors have signed an agreement to build such a railroad, and a Russian Jew has plans to develop more industry along the entire route. This will bring a lot of development to Samaria. However, this plan is presently not moving ahead. Professor Hillel Weiss started pushing for it about 30 years ago. He feels that when the next big war starts many more Jews will rush to Samaria because it is safer. This has already happened in previous wars.

Professor Hillel Weiss feels that there are still too many Jews, and even right-wing Zionists, who are too set on pleasing the President of the U.S. He said that Jews still have to overcome what many Jews succumbed to during the Holocaust. They compromised their Jewish identity to gain favors from the Nazis.

## Avri Ran

Avri Ran was a pioneer who crossed boundaries and lived "out of the box." He was not satisfied to live inside the fence of the new settlement of Itamar. Instead he moved to a hilltop beyond the settlement, and once enough other families moved with him to keep it going he would move on to another ridge to start another satellite settlement. The first ridge of several was only a mile away and was called "The Point."

Sharona Ran, the wife of Avri Ran, described what it was like when her husband left their home to capture his first hilltop. "He took a tent – actually just the lining of one – and went to the hilltop," said Sharona. "Our mode of communication was via a taxi radio. I would bring him food and equipment. It was a series of obstacles to get there, despite the not-so-distant location. We would spend the Sabbath there with a small generator. We began to sell our assets because we funded everything on our own. We sold two houses in Jerusalem and the farm in Beit Meir. Within a year there were four families living on 'The Point.'"

Ran then moved to the next hilltop, Hill 851, another mile further from the previous one along topographically difficult terrain. It could only be reached via tractor. He stayed there for a number of months until others joined him to settle the place. Then he continued forward.[24]

From the beginning Avri Ran began to develop an egg business. He established the satellite settlement of Givat Olam (Hills of the World) only three miles from the main Itamar settlement in late 1998.

Avri (short for Avraham) was born in 1955 in Nir Hen in the British Mandate of Palestine in what is now southern Israel. In 1994 Avri moved with his family to Itamar just ten years after the settlement started. The condition for them joining the community of Itamar was that they would be allowed to live outside the security fence and they would not be required to invest in the main community. Those living inside the fence in one of the rows of mobile homes would occasionally come outside the fence to visit, but only when they were armed.

Avri does not want to be against the settlers but he feels that the land needs to be settled without fences, barbed wire, and the army's protection. In contrast to other settlers he feels very strongly that they need to expand the area of the settlements as quickly as possible and to fill the area with more Jewish people. Even though the Jews are settling areas that are open and unused, the tendency is that once the Arabs realize that Jews

[24]HaLevi, Ezra. *Avri Ran, Father of the Hilltop Movement*. Israel National News. September 23, 2005.

are developing such land they will move as close to that area as possible to keep the Jewish settlement from expanding and to accuse the Jews of stealing land from the Arabs.

He feels that when the Russians migrated to Israel years ago they should have settled in Samaria and Judea, bringing millions of people. He thinks that even now the settlement movement would grow more if there were not such a high criteria for allowing families to join them. In the early stages of pioneering the settlements he had opposition from the Yesha Council and even Ariel Sharon, seemingly because he was developing settlements privately without the government's help or supervision. This opposition seemed strange and inconsistent to Avri, because for years many Jewish settlements in Israel have been the result of private enterprise. This is what he told them: "I am not your emissary. I am from the Land of Israel, and me and my sweet nation are doing things."[25]

Three years later, in 1997, after researching land ownership in the region, he pitched his tent on a hill four kilometers east of Itamar, which he was sure had no owner. One year later his wife, Sharona, and their children joined him. Sharona migrated to Israel with her family from the United States when she was four years old. They both were raised in secular Jewish homes, but have now become very religious and have ten children.

Unfortunately, in 1995 Avri was arrested and accused of assaulting local Arab residents who plowed with a tractor on land where Avri had planted crops. Actually, what really happened is that when the Arab tractor driver refused to leave, Avri pushed him and tore out the cables of his tractor. He was immediately apprehended by riot police and left-wing activists hiding where they could watch the whole ordeal.

Usually, if a Jewish settler has a problem it will take the police or army about 20 to 30 minutes to arrive, so there is no question that this was a set up. He was put under house arrest in a house that was not his own, but because it made it impossible to continue with his farming project he chose to leave the house

---

[25]Ibid.

arrest and did his best to avoid the law. Four months later, while vacationing with his family near the Jordan River, he was captured and jailed until the case came to court.

In January 2006, the judge acquitted Avri because the Arab testimony was evasive, and the land that Avri had farmed was clearly land that belonged to him. Avri's lawyer said that the Ta'ayush organization (Jews and Arabs against the Jewish Settlers) had organized the campaign against Avri. It seems odd that the government was on a hunt for Avri because, while he was establishing settlements, government leaders would come and discuss issues about the area and even spend the night with him. Even the Israeli army officers would come to him for advice when they were making decisions about the area.

Avri's wife told about one of the neighboring Arab villages, Yanoun, where the people did not really like Jews coming to the area. But they respected Avri because he was not afraid and understood how to deal with the Arabs. This resulted in a workable relationship until the left-wing people arrived on the scene. For example, the people of the Arab village of Yanoun would invite Avri to help them settle disputes among their people. Also, Avri would take water to them if they were short. If he had a problem with some of the Arabs, he would go directly to the Arab leaders to discuss it. Once he caught an Arab who had come to steal from him, and he immediately took the man to the leaders of the Arab community.

> There is a lot of state land in this area that lawfully belongs to the state of Israel, but if Jews do not come to live on that land then slowly the Arab neighbors will plant olive trees on the state land to try and claim it for themselves and eventually it becomes part of an Arab community. So the idea has been for the Jews to spread out as much as possible on all the hilltops and connect with the land by working the land, planting the land, and farming the land. This way no one, including the Israeli government, can uproot the Jewish settlers.[26]

---

[26]Passentin, Eliana. Deputy Director of Talmud Torah Hadar-Yosef. Author's recording during 2012 tour.

## Yigal Cohen-Orgad and the University in Samaria

During my interview with Yigal Cohen-Orgad, Chancellor of Ariel University, he explained the stages of the development of Ariel University. It began in 1982 when the College of Judea and Samaria was established to provide the area with an institution of higher education in the region. Its pioneers felt that establishing such an institution would help give some credence to the settlement movement in Samaria. It was also a response to show opposition to the Israeli government's forced evacuation of Jewish settlements

*Yigal Cohen-Orgad.*

in the Sinai. Originally the college operated as a regional branch of Bar-Ilan University in the settlement of Kedumim, but later was relocated in the larger city of Ariel. During 2004-2005 the school administration decided to become independent of Bar-Ilan and pursue university status.

From 1982 to 1986 the school ran evening courses mainly for residents of Samaria and the Jordan Valley. The college really started developing in 1987 when it opened its campus in the City of Ariel. Students from around the country were attracted to the college, and the number of students began to grow exponentially, with an ever-expanding range of departments opening and courses being offered.

In 2007 the College of Judea and Samaria was renamed Ariel University Center by a decision of the government. Under the new arrangement, the school entered a five-year period during which it underwent the examination of the Council for Higher Education to meet the high standards required. Government funding during this period was limited, although recognized undergraduate academic degrees equivalent to those from other institutions of higher education were granted. In 2012, at the end of this five-year period, and after a politically charged

*Ariel University cafeteria.*

public debate, the school was accredited and declared Israel's eighth full-fledged research university – the first university to be established in Israel in over 40 years.

When Yigal was hesitant about starting the college, he heard a statement by a professor older than himself at Hebrew University, who said, "The two-and-a-half tribes were exiled from east of the Jordan River only because they would not come to a place of learning. So if we want to develop Jewish resettlement of Samaria, we have to develop an institution of higher learning." This statement convinced Yigal to join in the effort to start an institution of higher education in the Shomron (Samaria). At that time Yigal did not live in Ariel, but did actually live in Samaria for 20 years from 1984 until 2004.

Many in Israel did not take the idea of a college in Samaria seriously. Even Cohen-Orgad thought it was unrealistic to think that students would ever come to Ariel from other parts of Israel for higher-level education. He knew that it would take a good number of students, lots of faculty, and departments. What he

*Ariel University library.*

did not take into consideration was the number of students who would be attracted to come from all parts of Israel. But the students did come, to the extent that students coming from outside the Samarian region now make up 85 percent of the enrollment, including Arab students from Jerusalem and as far away as the Galilee.

Throughout the years, the university has known times of struggle in its effort to gain full-university recognition. Not the least of these was dealing with two intifadas. Such times of trouble became a challenge to students from places like Haifa or Hadera getting to the school because of the security issues. Students from other parts of Israel had lots of other options for higher education. According to Cohen-Orgad, an Arab student coming from the Galilee area has the choice of ten institutions along the road to Ariel.

At first, there was mainly skepticism about an institute of higher learning in Samaria, but as it became apparent that a college in Samaria developed, the opposition began to grow.

The leader of this opposition was Yuli Tamir, former Minister of Education from the Labor Party. She fought to prevent the development of the College. Not only was she one of the founders of Peace Now, but she represented the views and the interests of the old establishment of the universities. She was a professor at another university and opposed starting any new university for four or five years. It is a miracle that this has happened because there have not been any other universities in any part of Israel for a long time.

All of these heroes help us to have a more complete picture of how the settlements started and all that has happened in Samaria as a result of the faith and courage of the Jewish settlers and all the Jews and Christians who have supported them.

# 6
# Life in Jewish Settlements of Samaria Today

In the previous chapters we have seen that the history and ownership of Israel today, especially the mountains of Israel, can be traced all the way back to early biblical history. This substantiates the Jews as the rightful owners of Judea and Samaria. However, we have seen how the Jews were forced to leave the land of their fathers, how Jews from abroad were allowed to start returning during the rule of the Ottoman Empire, and how the political situation finally made it possible, under God, for the modern nation of Israel to be reborn in 1948.

We have also seen how that God miraculously helped his people during three wars, both to survive and to gain land even though their enemies seriously outnumbered them. Finally, we have seen how the Jews began to return to Judea and Samaria, the heartland of Israel, after the Six-Day and Yom Kippur wars.

We need to keep in mind that the Jewish settlers and the settlements they founded in Judea and Samaria, like someone recently said, "are the Iron Dome for the rest of Israel." Judea and Samaria, as well as the Golan Heights, are all essential for the defense of Israel. And, the maps and charts in this book will help illustrate how important the Mountains of God are to all of Israel.

In this chapter it is time to take a closer look at the settlers, the settlements, and life today in Samaria. I am going to share with you through my own eyes and my own experience after having lived in Samaria for two years.

## City of Ariel

Ariel is already the largest so-called "settlement" in Samaria and is now classified as a town with a population of 20,000-plus. It is a thriving town with its own university, high school, middle school, four public primary schools, one religious primary school,

*View from university looking out over Ariel.*

medical clinics, a new performing arts center, a public swimming pool, a large membership gym and swimming pool, many synagogues, several large grocery stores, business complexes, and a large industrial park. The population swells by at least 15,000 or more when university students from all over the country are in town. It is always interesting to watch the traffic jam as the buses and cars arrive from all parts of Israel in time for morning classes.[1]

Ariel developed several factories to provide employment for the settlers in the local area, to eliminate the need to spend hours in buses commuting to work each day. In just ten years more than 30 percent of Ariel's work force has been employed locally. It was the policy of the Rural Administration that each new settlement should have a small industrial park to serve the community. So as part of this policy the Ministry of Trade and Commerce built a complex of 30 industrial units near the entrance to Ariel in 1981, just three years after the start of Ariel.

---

[1]See a video taken in Ariel in 2012
http://www.youtube.com/watch?v=AU4MhmXttVE

From the beginning, they planned on 300,000 square meters for industrial space, with as many as 6,000 workers employed in both the Ariel Industrial area and the Barkan Industrial plants, second only to Haifa. For their industrial zoning plan, Ariel was awarded the highest status by the government. Barkan was the first industrial complex in Samaria.

According to Natalie Hershkowitz, resident and advocate for the settlements, half or more of the workers in the Ariel and Barkan industrial complexes are Muslims. And, some of the Muslims have management positions over both Jews and Arabs. Jewish workers are rewarded each year with a paid vacation to the Red Sea resort town of Eilat for them and their families. An equal reward is available to the Muslim workers, who are provided a paid vacation to the Red Sea resort town of Aqaba in Jordan.

Ariel is mainly a Jewish community, but not exclusively. A number of local Arabs work in Ariel in construction, in the stores, and at the university. Non-Jews fill two prominent city positions; Ariel's city engineer is a Muslim Arab and the city treasurer is a Druze (monotheistic ethno religious community

*Barkan Industrial Park.*

distinct from the Muslim faith). In an earlier chapter I spoke about how the late founder and mayor, Ron Nachman, and the early settlers related well with their Arab neighbors. If not for those who still want to attack the Jews, the relationship would be even stronger than it is.

> Ron Nachman, blessed be his memory, dreamed of having a trans-Middle East railroad that would pass through both Ariel and nearby Nablus, and also an Ariel Regional Airport to serve both Jewish and Arab communities. He wanted to see the entire area developed for the benefit of all those living there no matter what their background or faith.[2]

## Ariel University

This university, with a current enrollment of 15,000 students, is the largest employer of Jews and Arabs in Samaria. It has had a significant impact on development in the area because of the jobs that it creates, and because it brings students from all over Israel to experience the beauty and the quiet of the mountains. As a result, some of the students decide to settle in Samaria rather than returning to other parts of Israel.

Another related benefit is an interesting development that has the university students living within a radius of 35 kilometers from Ariel. Because of limited dormitory space and other student housing, only about 4,000 students actually live in Ariel while attending school. This is also because of the high cost of housing in Ariel, due to the competition for what housing is available. As a result, some students have become like real estate agents. They have organized student villages in nearby settlements with more affordable housing in places such as Tapuach and Karnei Shomron. However, most of the students commute daily to and from Ariel from other areas in Israel.

Another way in which the university relates to the greater Samaria community is its arrangement with seven local yeshivas (religious learning centers for men) and three centers for women. This arrangement allows about 700 students to be able

---

[2]Zimmerman, Avi.

*Ariel University.*

to combine their religious studies with their academic studies.

Eldad Halachmi, Vice President of Resource Development at Ariel University, said that in addition to the 15,000 students there are 1,500 faculty and administrators. Ariel University is the fastest growing university in Israel, with 29 departments belonging to four faculties and two schools, four sections of faculties, and two schools including engineering, social sciences and humanities, health sciences, and one of the best schools of architecture in the country.

The university also has 15 research centers, including a cancer research center, a brain research center, a robotic and alternative energy research center. The Schlesinger Free Electron Laser Research Center attracts scientists from around the country to conduct their research. Many students shared with me about how friendly the faculty is, and that they really put a lot of personal effort into helping the students excel in their studies and research. One of the students from Netanya told me that his personal goal is to marry and raise his family in Samaria because

*Ariel University students.*

of the faith and high morals of the residents, compared to what his children would experience in many of the larger communities on the Mediterranean coast.

## Life in the Settlements

There are at least 40 settlements in Samaria alone, and when you add the number of settlements in the Jordan Valley, Binyamin, and Judea, that number swells to nearly 90. Many amazing things have developed in Judea and Samaria since 1967. In the following pages I want to write about various settlements in the Shomron, including descriptions of life in the settlements and input from individuals who live there, all coming from my interviews and visits during 2011 and 2012.

## The Settlement of Nofim

Over a two-year period, while living in Ariel while my wife was a student with a very special program at Ariel University, I drove much of Samaria and visited numerous settlements.

*Nofim community center.*

One of the settlements I visited was Nofim in Samaria, about a twenty-minute drive northwest of Ariel.

The settlement of Nofim is located in the beautiful mountains of Samaria, which is known by some as the Bible Belt of Israel. It is part of a block of settlements, including Havat Ya'ir, Yakir, Imanue'el, El Matan, Ma'ale Shomron, and Karnei Shomron. This growing community of 130 families and some 400 people is literally alive with people who are convinced that the hills and valleys of Samaria will again ring with the singing and prayers of the Jewish people.

As I drove toward the settlement to meet with the Secretary, Natalie Hershkowitz, I tried to imagine what it was like for the first settlers who made the drive as early as 1986, along a windy road from Petah Tikva, from the west, through the Arab villages. It was in 1986 when the Israeli government allowed a private company to lease state land, which is now the community of Nofim. One of the leaders of the community, Uzi Shimone, said that they have had very few problems with the Arabs. In fact the old highway was nicknamed "Hong Kong" highway because the local Arabs would line the highway, trying to sell produce and other wares to the Jewish settlers traveling through the area. The presence of Jews has benefited the local Arabs in the area. This picture summarizes the way in which Arabs from all over the Arab world have been attracted to the Land of Israel for the economic benefits of living near the Jews.

Uzi works on staff at Talpiot College of Education in Tel Aviv. The reason he lives in Nofim is that while living and working in Akko on the Mediterranean coast, a friend told him about the beauty of Nofim in Samaria. Immediately after visiting the area with his friend, he knew that this was where he wanted to live. Because of the recently constructed Highway 5, Trans-Samaria Highway, from Tel Aviv to Ariel, it only takes about twenty minutes for Uzi to drive west to Rosh HaAyin, where he then catches the train each day for work. He says that he is always relieved to get back home each evening to Nofim where it is so quiet and peaceful.

The community of Nofim is in a beautiful setting of

*Nofim community library.*

mountainsides covered with green bushes and olive trees. Peaceful relations with the Arabs in the area allow both citizens and visitors to hike trails in the Kana River Valley Reserve between Nofim and Yakir. Check out the references in the Bible to the Kanah Ravine, in Joshua 16:8 and 17:9. It was formally state land that was leased to a company in 1981 for the development of a Jewish community.

Eli has lived in Nofim for two years and is married with two children. He worked in the United States and other countries for several years, but is happy to be back in Israel and in Nofim.

The Nofim community workers' office also serves as the community library, which is open once a week. Hanna'ale, the community secretary, moved to Nofim 20 years ago because she was looking for a nice place to raise her children. Her oldest is now in university; her middle daughter is in the army and her youngest is in high school. Each school day a school bus takes her youngest and others to high school in the settlement of Ma'ale Efraim on the edge of the Jordan Valley, about a 30-kilometer drive from Nofim. Hanna'ale's duties include organizing all the weddings, funerals, holiday celebrations, and children's activities, including an afternoon program for children.

Another resident of Nofim, Ludmila, who comes from Russia, manages a large supermarket in Nofim that sells almost everything, including fresh vegetables and fruits. She and her family first lived in the settlement of Elon Moreh for seven years after making aliyah to Israel. Seventeen years ago, after friends told them about Nofim and the possibility of owning a home and property, they decided to make Nofim their home in 1995. Ludmila really likes the community and feels very comfortable and happy. She likes the combination of religious and secular families living together happily in the same community. It seems more like a city in which people truly have the freedom to decide how they want to live. Ludmila has two children and four grandchildren.

It always seems to please the parents when their children grow up and decide to remain in the community. I met Orit Natan,

*Nofim supermarket.*

who is a secretary and a student at Ariel University Center in Ariel, and she was kind enough to provide a good contact for me in Nofim. She is married with three children (two boys and one girl). Her parents arrived in Nofim in 1997. Currently one of the 69 new homes being built is for her and another is for her brother and his family.

The community growth has been in spurts. After growing to 100 families in 1997, there was not much growth or building for 15 years, but in 2012 many new homes were built. More property has been secured on which more homes will be built and the community hopes to attract more young couples. The community is a mixture of secular and religious and it is the religious who seem more interested in buying and building. They hope to see the community double in four or five years. The community is made up of professional people including doctors, professors, teachers, policemen, and others.

Along with the construction of new homes, a new beautiful community building was completed two years ago, which is

*The children's playground in Nofim.*

used for community gatherings and for the afternoon program for children. The room for the children is set up with several computers and a place for students to work on schoolwork. A new playground has recently been constructed as well. A big need is for a new kindergarten complex. Currently the kindergarten is using an old set of mobile homes. The workers and the children enjoy wonderful learning activities but are hoping for funds for a new building.

These people of faith fit so well in the setting of the mountains of Samaria. Hopefully no enemy force or the government of Israel will be able to uproot such beautiful people and communities that have been planted there by God's providential hand.

## The Settlement of Itamar

My first contact with Itamar came in May of 2011 when I visited with Hadassah, a young mother from Itamar who was selling things at a concession booth during Israel's independence celebration at the Israeli army base, Bad Shalosh. This came only a few months after the horrific murder of the Fogel parents and three of their children in March of that same year, by Palestinian terrorists, which alarmed much of the world. I asked Hadassah about the impact of this horrible event on her and the community. She responded with a cheerful look on her face saying:

> I believe that God can even take this tragedy and work good out of it. Since then the love that people have for each other has grown and the community feels closer to each other and are even more determined to see their community grow.

She said that the government has given permission for more houses to be built. The residents in Itamar have built a new synagogue named after Udi Fogel, the father slain by the terrorists. Hadassah was extremely positive that God is still in control. I came away awestruck by the quality of these Jewish settlers and the level of their faith.

This was also reinforced by my first visit to Itamar itself a few months later, in August of 2011, when I interviewed Moshe Goldsmith, Mayor of Itamar, and his wife, Leah, for this book. It was a sunny, pleasant day as I drove the 20 miles from Ariel north on Highway 60 toward Shechem (Nablus), through the Arab community of Huwara to Highway 5077 that took me east to Itamar.

Itamar was established in 1984, with 12 families, and has now grown to more than 200 families, with paved roads, nicely built homes, schools, a yeshiva, organic farms, and synagogues. They have a yeshiva high school for boys and another yeshiva for young men who have completed high school. Many young people from other parts of Israel come and study for two years before starting their compulsory military service.

Moshe and Leah felt drawn to Israel and moved there just a year after Itamar was started. They wanted not only to live in Israel, but also to live in a settlement. After searching for a place to live for a year, they were thrilled to find a small settlement that was just starting. After they made some visits and got acquainted with the ten residents, they decided to move there. Initially they drove dirt roads to the settlement and lived in a singlewide mobile home with only a generator for power that gave lights for just a few hours each evening. Water was piped in from a source in the valley, but the Arabs kept cutting the lines and stealing water. Moshe completed his rabbinic education in a nearby settlement and is now a rabbi in Itamar and teaches in a school for boys that he started.

*Moshe and Leah Goldsmith.*

Leah Goldsmith said about living in Itamar:

My husband and I came to the land to pioneer and to have a connection with our spiritual roots in the central part of Israel that is the actual heart of Israel. We have been blessed to live here. Every day I get to look out my window at the valley of Joseph, you must remember Joseph in the Bible, and a little to the left is the resting place of Itamar and Eleazar, sons of Aaron the High Priest. And if you look up on the mountain you will see the resting place of Gideon whose story is in the book of Judges.

I mention these people because so many people have heard of them because the Bible is the most sold book in the world. I have one son named Joseph and another son named Ephraim. Jews all over the world, no matter where they live, name their children after these people in the Bible. I just want to share with you where these people are from and that they are from my backyard so to speak.

If you are wondering why I am living here it is because

*Itamar neighborhood.*

this is the most natural thing for us to do to live in the land where Jacob purchased land and then where later the children of Israel buried the bones of Joseph. When the Jews entered the land under Joshua they came to Shechem between Mount Gerizim and Mount Ebal. Thank God we are here and have taken over beautiful land that lay barren and desolate for 2,000 years and have turned it into something green and productive. This is a fulfillment of all that our prophets wrote about how God would collect His people and gather them back to the land their original land that includes places like Jerusalem, Hebron, and Shechem.[3]

Moshe has been on the ruling council of Itamar for 16 years and is now the mayor of the community. In 2001, before a security fence was constructed some boys playing basketball at the high school were attacked and killed by Arab terrorists. As a result, many thought that they might have to close the school, but to everyone's surprise the parents kept sending their children and the school tripled in size. Many parents from other communities

---

[3] *The Spring of Judea and Samaria.*

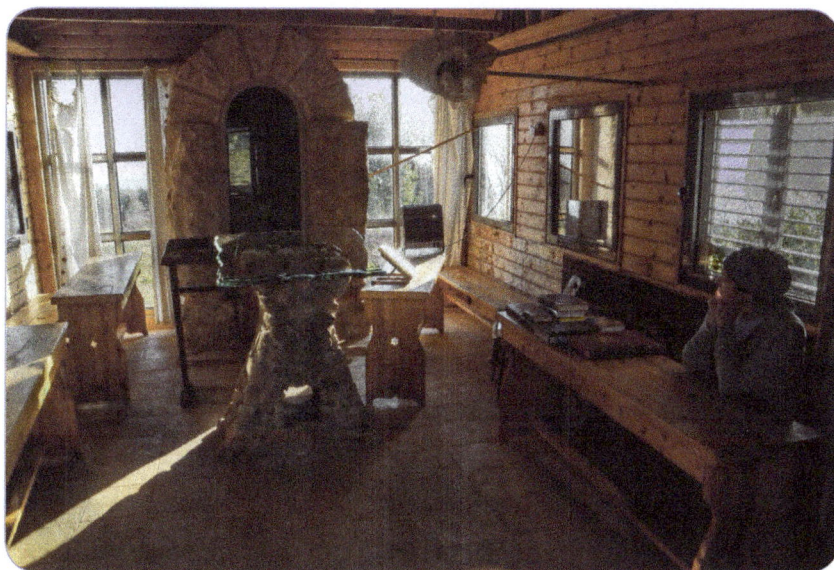

*Itamar synagogue.*

are now sending their children to learn in Itamar because they have teachers and schools that cater to special-needs children. Even though Itamar has suffered much injury and loss of life from the hands of terrorists, it continues to grow and expand.

Many of the students from the 18 graduating classes who have gone on to serve in the army and attend university have also married and returned to settle in Itamar, and other settlements, to continue with their professions. Many young men also come to attend one of the two yeshivas to gain spiritual preparation for their service in the army. Soon girls will also be able to attend a yeshiva for them, called Beit Yaakov (House of Jacob). They plan this for the high school level as well as the higher education level. In Itamar as in all Jewish religious schools, at all levels of education the Bible is taught.

It is a miracle that Itamar has grown as much as it has because of restrictions on building and the difficulty of living there during the intifada. Avri Ran pioneered the development of the greater Itamar area, and now these communities are part of the Itamar Neighborhood. You can read more about him in the previous chapter, "Samaria Settlement History and Pioneers".

Itamar is not just what a person sees when they drive through the main gate, but also includes communities in an area of 12 square kilometers.

I have visited the Alomot Farm just a few miles from the main settlement of Itamar. This farm, operated by the Mishuami family, is always developing something new, including the recent addition of cattle and goats resulting in delicious goat cheese. They are planting more and more olive trees and grape vineyards. They work so hard on the farm that they have not had time yet to build themselves a proper home.

The Alomot Farm is near the Givat Arnon farm, also called 777 because of its elevation. It features a breathtaking panorama view of the Jordan Valley and the surrounding area, which is unforgettable. Much development results from the tragic deaths caused by terrorist attacks because, as stated before, the Jewish settlers do not react to terrorism with defeat, but instead with more determination, expansion, and building. This was the case

*Olive trees at Itamar.*

*Goats at the Givat Olam farm.*

with the 777 community and farm that was started in memory of Arye Agranioni who was murdered here in 2001 while guarding the outpost.

Not far from the previous two farms is Givat Olam, another hilltop farm that is now one of the largest organic farms in Israel. It produces and sells organic eggs, goat's milk, raspberry, peach, date, and blueberry yogurt, grain for wheat, free-range chickens, garlic and dill, and Bulgarian cheese from sheep and goats. The owners have placed a piano in the goat shed in order to have music while the goats are milked. But more important, they also have high quality equipment for their farming itself!

This farm is owned and run by Avri Ran, who was the pioneer and settlement hero of this area as detailed previously. Sarah, one of his daughters who is married and works on the farm, told me in my interview with her that about 50 young people from all over Israel have been attracted by Avri's brave pioneering and have come to live and work on the farm from six months to five years at a time. Many troubled young people have been welcomed and helped in a positive way while working and living with the Rans. Avri is like a father to these troubled youth.

*Givat Olam Organic Yogurt.*

He built the farm itself little by little, with his personal funds and without protection from the Israeli army or police. And even today you will not see any fences around these hilltops. Only Jewish Zionist labor is used on the farm, which is a principle that he feels very strongly about because it helps keep the spiritual connection with the land.

> The land must not be sold permanently, because the land is mine and you are but aliens and my tenants. Throughout the country that you hold as a possession, you must provide for the redemption of the land.
>
> (Leviticus 25:23-24)

It is what can be called Gush Itamar. Itamar grew to 40 families by 2001, but the terrible murders starting in 2000 and on through 2004 was not an easy time and caused the growth to slow down.

It has not been easy for the people living in Itamar. Terrorists have murdered 16 of their residents over the years. One terrible example occurred when a mother with small children was at home preparing food for Shabbat when a terrorist entered her home and shot and killed her and her three children. The people continue on because they know that God has given the Jews this land as an inheritance, and that building the land will never be easy. They also realize that it calls for a sacrifice to do what God wants. They are sad and they cry, but at the same time they smile and are happy because of the growth and the new communities. When the people have a strong faith, nothing deters them from growth and development.

Moshe's rabbi and teacher, Binyamin Herling, was murdered while leading some hikers up Mount Ebal October 19, 2000. While they were praying, snipers came out from the nearby Arab village of Ascar and started firing. The one security person with the rabbi and the hikers was not a match for hundreds of rifles. The rabbi was hit by a bullet and bled to death. The Israeli helicopter that was sent to transport him to the hospital could not land in time because many people were there and the crew was afraid that landing so close to these people would cause even more injuries.

Following the murder of Rabbi Binyamin Herling, Moshe was motivated to go on with his life and teaching. People often ask him why he would stay in the West Bank when there have been many horrific murders of 22 people including that of his rabbi during a ten-year period. But his answer is very much like that of the other settlers. They know that they are called to build the Land of Israel and that sometimes they have to pay the ultimate price for it, but they will never give up. They know that God has given them the land as an inheritance for the Jews. They are following the words of the Torah and are building a future for the Jewish nation.

Following many attacks during the intifada, Itamar became like a ghost town for a period of time with little or no growth, but after that period they added 60 families. At the time of this writing there are more than 200 families, or about 1300 people. As the Jewish population grows, so does the Arab population. There seems to be competition. Jews were hindered from growth by the building freeze while the Arabs just keep building illegally.

The more Arab houses there are, the more room that is created for Arabs, but there is insufficient housing for all the young Jewish families who want to move to Samaria. The population of the Arab villages also continues to grow.

It seems quite peaceful to drive around Samaria through Arab villages and Jewish settlements, but in fact there is still trouble. During the week that I conducted interviews someone was driving up a mountain to have a good view of Joseph's Tomb and Arabs threw rocks and broke his windshield. Also, a woman was driving at night and two Arabs stopped her car and stole it. Then a young man was hitchhiking not far from Ariel when a car stopped and gave him a ride. He thought it was okay because the men in the front seat were both wearing kippas (traditional Jewish head covering), but once he was seated in the back seat he realized that he was in an Arab car and that they were trying to kidnap him. He managed to open the door and jump out before they could stop him.

In the past things were much safer. The people of Itamar and other communities would have their cars repaired in Shechem (Nablus) and would even use the post office there. It was so safe that they would leave their cars unlocked when shopping and buying groceries. It got worse after the so-called peace talks started. However, it was not the Jews who severed relations with the Arabs; it was the other way around. Currently, some Jews do business with the Arabs but it is not good for Arabs to relate to Jews because, as soon as they do, they are in jeopardy with the more radical Arabs. The Arabs threaten to murder their own people for dealing with the Jews.

A few months later, on Israel's Tu B'Shevat (Israel's tree planting day), I visited Itamar again. While there, trees were being planted in memory of the Fogel family members who were murdered. There were even young people who came from other parts of Israel to remember the Fogel family by planting a tree. The planting of hundreds of trees is one of the many ways in which Jews remember those who have died.

I again visited Itamar for the first *yahrtzeit* (the anniversary of

*Yeshiva in memory of Udi Fogel.*

the death of a loved one) for the Fogel family. It was a stormy, windy, rainy day, but the community of Itamar was filled with joy and thanksgiving because of how God had blessed them since the murder of members of the Fogel family. It was a yahrtzeit for the family and a dedication of the new yeshiva and synagogue in memory of murdered father, Udi Fogel. People came from all over Judea and Samaria and other parts of Israel too. It was surprisingly a very festive occasion, much of which took place in the home where members of the Fogel family were murdered. The Jews were very excited, not about the murder, but about all that God is doing to turn evil into good. The rabbis and scribes also completed the writing of the new Torah scroll for the synagogue on the day of this celebration and then marched with the new scroll from the Fogel house to the new synagogue to place it in the ark of the new yeshiva as part of a dedication service of the synagogue.

A short time later I visited Itamar again with a friend, to learn more about the farming that is taking place. You may remember that I wrote about how the Jews were required to choose mountaintops for their communities so as not to disturb the Arabs who were living and farming in the fertile valleys. Because the mountaintops are so rocky and lack water they were the most unlikely place to expect any success with agriculture, but the opposite is true. For example, Rachel and Alon Zimmerman, who have been farming in Itamar since the founding of the community in 1984, showed us what they have done. Initially they produced tomatoes for export, but they learned to adjust as the economic and political situation changed. For example, during the security problems of the first and second intifada it was difficult to transport the vegetables to the market. That time of difficulty, when they had so many fruits and vegetables they couldn't sell, led them to making jelly, spreads, vegetable sauces, and fruit leather that they still make and sell today.

Recently, they have been experimenting with hydroponics, which is growing vegetables without soil. Alon explained that his project is really better called aquaponics, because the water comes from a large fish tank that holds 100 kilograms of live fish and is sufficient for growing them. The waste products of the fish are enough to support a thousand plants. After a process of nitrification the water is sent to the plants, which removes the nitrogen and purifies the water, which then flows back to the fish tank via gravitation. The entire project takes only five cubic meters of water that is continually recycled.

Their goal is to grow vegetables like lettuce free of insects, so that it will be kosher, and to grow it without pesticides. The water prevents most insects that are normally in the soil from reaching the lettuce plants. The mesh that is used to cover beds with plants prevents most insects from getting to the plants from the topside. Alon also has some other ways to protect the plants without using any pesticides. Overall the whole project is more ecologic than organic.

Rachel continues to produce many kinds of cheese, dried fruit leather, yogurt, granola, and more from their farm. They have found that, to survive as farmers, they must lower the cost of growing and then go directly to the consumer – and encourage the consumers to come directly to them – to make enough profit to support them and keep their projects going. Alon says that much of the farming is still in the experimental stage, but if it really proves successful they could easily produce up to 10,000 plants without adding any more fish.

Overall it is a very economical system, but the beds for the plants are a big expense initially. One of the benefits is that there is no weeding required and the farmer can stand up rather than bend over to care for the plants and to harvest them.[4]

I drove some friends visiting from the United States to Itamar in February 2012, while showing them the Shomron, and we had a wonderful lunch in a new restaurant in a Jewish home just outside the main settlement of Itamar. This special Jewish couple had recently opened their restaurant in their home, affording a marvelous view of Shechem nestled between Mount Gerizim and Mount Ebal. These Jews are known as the happy Jews! They have migrated to this area from the Galilee. The husband, who is the cook, showed us his happiness as he entertained us with his amazing piano playing and singing.[5]

Overall, this area is attracting more and more tourists who come to see the farms and buy cheese, yogurt, eggs, and other products. They also like to enjoy the quiet, fresh air and the amazing views from places like the Three Seas Observation Point, which on a clear day affords a view of the Mediterranean Sea, the Dead Sea, and the Sea of Galilee.

## The Settlement of Elon Moreh

Elon Moreh is mentioned in the Bible as the place where Abraham stopped to view the Land as he made his initial visit.

On a beautiful day in January 2011 I departed from Ariel descending from its high elevation along a new direct highway to

---

[4]Goldsmith, Moshe. YouTube Video Interview with Alon Zimmerman, 2012. http://www.youtube.com/watch?v=4ARbjg1gABs

[5]If you would like to see a video I took of this, you can use this web address: http://www.youtube.com/watch?v=gxG1hS4_Uw0

*Upper Elon Moreh.*

Highway 60, also known as Highway of the Patriarchs: Abraham, Isaac, and Jacob. After two miles I came to the tee-junction with Highway 60 and passed the settlement of Rechelim and then went north to what is called Tapuach Junction where Highway 60 intersects with Highway 505 near Kfar Tapuach. I continued another three miles on Highway 60 driving through the Arab village of Huwara where no one seemed to notice me driving along because the Arabs were busy shopping and conducting their business. Highway 60 has a lot of traffic with an equal number of Arab and Jewish vehicles. It is possible to tell because the Arabs have white license plates while the Israeli plates are yellow.

I turned off Highway 60 shortly before the ancient town of Shechem, which the Arabs call Nablus.[6] I continued east/

---

[6]The Romans renamed Shechem as Annapolis, after the Roman city Neapolis, which later became known as Naples, Italy. But because the Arabs have trouble pronouncing a "p", "Neapolis" ended up being pronounced as "Nablus."

*Entrance road to Elon Moreh.*

northeast on Highway 557 toward Elon Moreh, passing the turnoff to the settlement of Itamar and then climbed up to Elon Moreh, which is at a higher elevation than Ariel and in a very beautiful setting.

The last part of the drive, toward the entrance to Elon Moreh, goes through a beautiful tunnel like area formed by the branches of a pine tree forest that have been planted over the years. Elon Moreh is at the base of Mount Kabir, which is believed to be the mountain that Abraham stood on when he first came into the land. This mountain affords a marvelous view of Mount Gerizim and Mount Ebal as well as the city of Shechem.

I learned so much about Elon Moreh from my interview with Gershon Portnoy and from having him show me around. Gershon is a certified tour guide and is one of the best for showing this area.

This attractive community is made up of some 300 families and has an estimated population of 3,000. It seems that each section of new housing in Elon Moreh is on a higher level than the original part of the town. This proved to be quite interesting in that, after I had driven through the gate I stopped and used my cell phone to ask Gershon for directions to his home. Once he knew the color of my car he talked to me all the way to his house telling me to turn this way or that. He lived high enough that he could see me the whole time. And, after I arrived and looked out his window at what he could see, I was amazed.

Gershon and I sat at the dining room table with a cup of tea and some other treats as I interviewed him to learn about Elon Moreh.

According to the Bible, Elon Moreh is where this is recorded:

> Abram traveled through the land as far as the site of the great tree of Moreh at Shechem. At that time the Canaanites were in the land. The Lord appeared to Abram and said, "To your offspring I will give this land." So he built an altar there to the Lord, who had appeared to him.
>
> (Genesis 12:6-7)

Elon Moreh was started in 1980 by ten families, and it is now a well-established, authorized settlement. However, according to some people's political perspective it is still unauthorized. Remember, the Garin Elon Moreh Two was given permission to

*Elon Moreh.*

move to this location because it was state land and not private Arab land.

The residents of Elon Moreh do not have any personal animosity toward individual Arabs according to what the Torah teaches about relationships with all people, but Jews do not deny the struggle they have with Arab nations. If a nation or a village conducts acts of terror or carries on acts of anti-Semitism then Jews will respond in self-defense. However, adults teach their children to not hate individual Arabs generally because of the acts of a few. Jews have personal, individual contact with Arabs such as at gas stations and shops. It is the western media that likes to portray all Jews as hating and mistreating all Arabs.

The community of Elon Moreh is made up of religious Jewish families, and a central committee of five makes the decisions concerning the affairs of the community. The only workers paid by the community are one outside government person and some non-Jewish foreign workers.

At a special gathering, when people were questioned as to why they came to live in Elon Moreh, the Jews spoke of their ideology, the people who live here, and because this is the biblical heartland. When one of the foreign workers was asked why he was there, he said it was because he was able to have such a good job.

Elon Moreh was started in 1980, seven years after the Yom Kippur War of 1973. This was 13 years after Israel gained control of the area during the Six-Day war in 1967, while defending themselves against attack from the neighboring Muslim countries. Elon Moreh was established about 33 years ago by an ideological nucleus which – as explained previously – is called a "Garin." The initial nucleus included strong people with faith and a pioneering spirit who were willing to live in tents and mobile homes, using generators for power and surviving on the absolute basics of life. The settlement has expanded upward from its original location so that now the housing covers the entire hill. People are still living in some of the original mobile homes, but most of those original homes are now quite old and hard to live in.

The beautiful pine tree forest on the lower part of the settlement was planted by the Jewish National Fund to show that this was truly state land that belonged to the Jews, and to keep the Arabs from squatting on the land to claim it for themselves. This was done before the settlement started. Now, even though the settlers are living in Elon Moreh and developing it, their eventual goal of settling in Shechem has not changed. They believe that one day, by God's divine help, this will happen. It is important for Jews to control the area around Joseph's Tomb.[7]

Gershon told me that he migrated to Israel in 1978, from Florida, and attended Bar Ilan University, where he studied political science. He had visited Israel a couple of times before he migrated, and because he had a longing for the land he returned to live in Israel. He no longer felt at home in the U.S.

After he was at the university for a year, he lived on a kibbutz in Beit She'an for a month before serving in the Israeli army for three years. He then studied in a yeshiva for three years before getting married. After his marriage, he and his wife lived in Jerusalem for a year-and-a-half, but while in the army he also lived in Shiloh for another year-and-a-half, which gave him the desire to live in Judea and Samaria.

After living in Jerusalem, Gershon and his wife lived in Cochav Yaakov in Binyamin for two years and then moved to Elon Moreh in 1990 with one child. Since moving to Elon Moreh they have added five more children to their family.

Today Elon Moreh has a major scroll-producing company, a Salami factory, a very important mobile home factory that provides housing especially for Jews in the newer settlements, a clinic, a supermarket, two elementary schools, grades one through eight, one for boys and one for girls, a high school, a post office, and a community swimming pool.

Regarding schooling in the settlements, the custom is that students do not attend high school in the same settlement

---

[7]The United Nations Relief organization has 30,000 paid workers who do not want to lose their jobs, which would happen if the Palestinian refugee issue is resolved.

that they live in. So the Elon Moreh children go to school in a different location south of the settlement. They board there some nights, but are bused back and forth other days of the week. The same thing is true of children from other settlements, as they are bused to the high school in Elon Moreh.

On the subject of Jewish children in the settlements being bused to schools away from their own community, this may raise some questions in the mind of the reader. Transporting school children is fairly secure because of the use of bulletproof buses and the current security on the roads.

The main reason why parents choose to have their children transported to schools not in their community is that the various schools have differences in style of teaching and some have higher religious standards which are expressed in a demand for more modest dress codes – though in contrast with western standards – all of the high schools for girls in Samaria are very modest. Even on this matter, among the Jewish communities there are slight differences, significant enough for some parents to prefer one school to another.

Another reason for parents to choose a school in a different community is the size of classes; obviously there are some parents who prefer to send their kids to a school where the classes are smaller.

Students have lots of choices as to where they can attend school. Some choose to attend high school in Jerusalem and others choose to attend a regional high school. There is also a large yeshiva in Elon Moreh. The three synagogues provide worship for Ashkenazi, Sephardic, and Yemenite attendees respectfully.

Public buses operate two times each day to Jerusalem for those who work there or need to go there for their education. Also, once every hour there is a bus to and from the Tapuach Junction, where people hitch a ride to other centers. Highway 557 to Itamar and Elon Moreh was built only about nine years ago. Before that, the residents would drive to Shechem and then take Highway 60 toward Ariel or Jerusalem, but due to the trouble during the intifada, and the danger of driving through a heavily Arab population center, the decision was made to build a new highway.

A young entrepreneur was so determined to see industry develop locally that he started the mobile home factory. He is what Jews call a "bulldozer" person (datfor). He employs about 60 people. He is also now into conventional construction, building stick homes in the settlements.

Elon Moreh is home of a good-sized almond tree farm, and grape vineyards. This settlement also has a nice area for housing guests that includes a dining room and is able to host about 100 people at a time for courses or for Bar Mitzvahs and other gatherings.

For 20 years a Torah-scroll factory in Elon Moreh has prepared skins for the Torah to be written on for synagogues. Most of the meat in Israel is imported from Argentina and China, and there is an agreement that these kosher meat places in Argentina and China will send calf fetuses to Israel to produce Torah scrolls. The skin factory in Elon Moreh is now the largest Torah skin factory in Israel.

The preparation stages are rather interesting. The first time I visited the factory I was amazed at all they have to do before the skins are ready for a Jewish scribe, called a Sopher, to write the Torah on it for a synagogue. First, they wash the skins with chemicals to clean them of any hair or meat and they wash off the chemicals and dry them. The washing also softens them and gives them a little whitening. Second, they wet the skins again and place them on stretching racks. Third, they refine the skin with an electric sander and then they cut the skins to the proper size for a scribe. The skin is also used for mezuzahs for doorways. The mezuzah contains the Shema, which is a prayer from the Torah and is placed on the doorways of Jewish homes.

Many people still have to commute from Elon Moreh each day for work in other places due to a lack of sufficient work locally. New homes are being built and more people are being attracted to live in Elon Moreh and other areas of Samaria. As long as the

*Torah skin factory.*

Israeli government does not interfere or hinder, I believe that there will be continuing growth in the Jewish population. A lot of Jews are attracted to the quieter and peaceful communities away from the larger cities.

## The Settlement of Ma'ale Efraim

Technically, the settlement of Ma'ale Efraim is part of the Jordan Valley settlements, but it is quite close to other settlements in Samaria, and the people of Samaria visit there often.

On our way to the Dead Sea, Charlotte and I stopped to visit a family in the settlement, which overlooks the beautiful Jordan Valley along Highway 505. This was our first contact with the settlement and the family.

## A Ma'ale Efraim Family

The husband works for a winery in another settlement, Rechelim, and he and his wife have three lovely children. At the time of our meeting they had lived in Ma'ale Efraim for only six months. After their marriage they moved to the small settlement of Yafit in the Jordan Valley, initiating an agricultural project. The husband has a degree in agriculture and had a dream of starting his own agricultural project. He acquired a number of grape vines and hoped to develop a winery. He was soon growing other produce as well, on four acres of land, but after five years they decided to move to Ma'ale Efraim because they felt the need for living in a larger community with schools for their children. Also they wanted a community with a synagogue where they could worship and study each day. They feel that it is only the Torah that gives the Jews the right to be settling in Samaria. Because of his education and experience he is now an asset to the winery he is working for.

The religious and secular relate together so well in Ma'ale Efraim. They said that, as a contrast, in Jerusalem there seems to be quite a barrier between the secular and the religious. They said that 80 percent of the population of Israel is reported to have faith, but even though they may think about God they really do not have the kind of faith that affects how they live their lives.

The wife mentioned that she learned about many different cultures and religions in school. She said that the secular Jews tend to be more pro Arab and live in opposition to the Jews who are living in the settlements because of their faith in the Bible and what it says about the heartland of Israel. She really has not related to Arabs before or after becoming religious. Even though you can see both Arabs and Jews in the same shops and riding the same buses in cities like Jerusalem, there is generally not a congenial relationship between the two groups, because the Arabs in Jerusalem seem hostile toward Jews according to her. She said that one exception might be the coastal city of Haifa,

*Ma'ale Efraim.*

where Jews and Arabs seem to relate rather well with each other. This shows that a good relation between the two groups really is possible, but Jews are not going to give up their right to the land.

She said that in Samaria the Arabs have free water and electricity, but they do not serve in the army or pay taxes. And yet, at the same time they steal animals, crops, and cars from the Jews. There was more stealing going on in Yafit than in Ma'ale Efraim; because of its size, Ma'ale Efraim has better security. They said that although the Israeli government could have annexed Judea and Samaria in 1967, now the issues are more complicated and get more complicated as time goes on. They feel that Jews need to know who they are and should not try to assimilate with all the cultures around them. One of the problems is that religious Jews see too much of other cultures on television, and then tend to move away from their own Jewishness.

## Ma'ale Efraim Community Coordinator

I was also able to have an interview with Ronit Cohen,

Community Coordinator for Ma'ale Efraim. She explained that Ma'ale Efraim is large enough to have their own government council, making them independent of the Jordan Valley or Shomron Council. This is also true of the city of Ariel. The Israeli government and other leaders felt that this ridge of the Jordan Valley where Ma'ale Efraim is situated was such an ideal place for a settlement that they built large homes to attract wealthy Jews, hoping that that would help the settlement become a very prosperous community serving as a main center for the military. It was called "The Pearl of the Shomron." The result was that many people were drawn to the community initially, but that has changed as the economy has caused living here to be more expensive. Initially people were hoping that Ma'ale Efraim would become a tourist attraction because of its location and the beauty of the area, but any such result has been slow to develop. However, there are still some nice bed and breakfast businesses.

She told us that Ma'ale Efraim is a community of 400 families, or about 2,000 people. The population is a mixture of religious and secular Jews, and even a few non-Jews. This community was first established in 1978, with encouragement from the Israeli government, yet it has only 80 religious families, while 320 families are secular or traditional.

She took us to a brand new outdoor adult exercise park. These exercise parks are now all over Israel. In Israel it is no longer only children who play in the parks, but also the adults now go to the parks for exercise. She also took us inside their community center, which had a first-class exercise gym including exercise machines and weights and a full-sized swimming pool. She showed us the high school where more than 200 students from all over Samaria and the Jordan Valley attend. The business center includes two medical clinics, a large grocery store, a gas station and a very unique second-hand store where people volunteer to help with stocking and operating. In this shop nothing is sold, but people who have a need simply come and help themselves once a week to clothing, shoes, electronic items, kitchen items, and books. The industrial section is growing and providing more local

*Ma'ale Efraim adult outdoor exercise park.*

employment. Ma'ale Efraim headquarters the police station for this part of Samaria and Jordan Valley. The large army base near the settlement enhances security.

There is one preschool for infants, two kindergartens, and two clubs for kids from the first grade to the sixth grade divided by age groups where the children can come after school and stay until six in the evening to get help with school work, learn various crafts, fun activities, and are served a hot meal. Volunteers work with the children as a help to the parents who are working and the families that have financial needs. The community is also trying to restart a petting zoo they had in the past. One of the reasons it was closed was because of a problem with foxes getting through the fence and killing the peacocks and other animals. There are plans to start this up again, but they will need to improve the fence. One of the purposes of the petting zoo was for the youth to learn how to take care of the animals. There are 300 youth of all ages in the community.

New homes are now being built for the first time in 13 years.

The company *Amana* built homes here about 13 years ago. The Binyanei Bar Amana Construction and Development Company is building the new homes in Ma'ale Efraim, which is the primary construction company for the settlements. They prefab the house in their factory and then deliver it partially constructed. This is being done in many of the settlements and is a big help because there is a great shortage of housing, which hinders the growth of the settlements. When we visited with Ronit there was no room for new families who might want to come, and the situation will not change until more homes are built. For years there was plenty of room, but suddenly the town filled to capacity, which caused rents to increase. In the past, rents were low enough for students attending university in the city of Ariel to live in Ma'ale Efraim and commute back and forth.

The synagogue is a Sephardic synagogue with a Chabad rabbi, but of course all Jews are welcome there including Sephardic, Ashkenazi, and Yemenite Jews. At this stage the community has

*Ma'ale Efraim business plaza.*

*Ma'ale Efraim high school.*

decided to have just one synagogue that is open to everyone rather than having multiple synagogues. Separate from the synagogue is a yeshiva with its own synagogue for the students. There is also a kind of special yeshiva that prepares young men spiritually for the army.

One reason why this description of Ma'ale Efraim is so important is that facilities, activities, modern homes, paved roads, and the people who live there are typical of all the settlements, although some are small and some are large. Meeting the settlers and seeing what has happened in a relatively short amount of time is again evidence of the blessing that God has given these people.

## The Settlement of Gilad Farm

I was able to visit Gilad Farm on the occasion of their tenth anniversary, and at other times as well. Even though Gilad Farm was started on land legally purchased from Arabs by Moshe Zar, whose son, Gilad, was murdered by terrorists not far from where the settlement of Gilad Farm is located today, there are those who are opposed to this settlement.

The heroes of this settlement have struggled to have electricity and water because of the lack of support from the Israeli government. But this community, which is centered on God, its synagogue, and its yeshiva, continues to expand and develop. On one visit I was guided around the community by an enthusiastic group of young school-age children. I was impressed that so many of the families are raising their own chickens, ducks, and sheep.

This settlement is too small for a grade school or high school, but they do have a wonderful kindergarten and nursery school. They also have a synagogue and host a yeshiva for young men from other communities who come to study the Torah. Several times I have visited with Yehuda Shimon, who works each day as a lawyer in Jerusalem but lives in Gilad Farm with his wife, Elana, and his seven children, where he also serves as the chairman of the community. Yehuda and his wife are dedicated to the development of the settlement with the other 28 families. They see themselves as the children of Abraham, Isaac, and Jacob.

*Gilad Farm.*

Their goal is to see more homes and more children and the hills alive with trees and produce.

## The Settlement of Har Bracha

During my two years living in Ariel I made several visits to beautiful Har Bracha (Mountain of Blessing), named after the mountain on which it is situated. This mountain is also known as Mount Gerizim. When the community of Har Bracha was started in 1984 there was nothing here except a few trees, rocks, and wild animals roaming around. The Israeli government brought in 30 prefabbed homes for the 15 families who came to start the community. This meant that another 15 homes were vacant, so people from nearby communities were asked to come and volunteer for a year to help get things started.

After the first year, when the volunteers started returning to their original places, for various reasons others also started leaving until there was only one family left on the mountain, with four soldiers guarding them. Thankfully that same family is still living in Har Bracha today, and they really did not mind living there on their own for a few years until other folks began to come and join them. The community did grow after that setback, and now about 300 families are living there with a total population of about 2,000. The size of the average family is between four and five children, and some of the older families have 10 to 12 children.

The renewed growth is largely due to Rabbi Eliezer Melamed, who started a yeshiva in the Har Bracha settlement in 1992. In 1987 some religious Jews in Jerusalem, who could not bear to see so many empty houses in Har Bracha – and because they were afraid the community might not succeed – sent several young families from Jerusalem to live there. After this happened a celebration was organized for Har Bracha, which attracted many families and friends of those who had just taken up residence. This actually resulted in others deciding to move to the community.

After the community grew to 13 families they decided that they needed a rabbi. Rabbi Melamed from Beit El, under whom

*Har Bracha Yeshiva.*

some of the residents had studied before moving to the Har Bracha settlement, was invited to come for a visit on a Shabbat (Saturday). During that Shabbat, when the rabbi walked around the housing area (which offered very little to see), he said that he thought that he could bring some fresh ideas to the community that would help it to grow. He was not just talking about teaching new insights into the Torah, but ideas that would bring the community schools, kindergartens, synagogues, and much more.

As a result he started the town's yeshiva, which attracted young men from other parts of Israel to study. However, they did not spend all of their time studying, but instead spent half of it in the army. These men turned out to be some of the best soldiers because their training in the yeshiva that helped them understand their proper role in the land. They understood their Jewish roots and thus understood why they were in the land and why they needed to defend it. The wonderful result of all of this is that after their schooling and time in the army, many of

*Inside Har Bracha Yeshiva.*

them decided to return to the Har Bracha settlement with their wives and settle down, raise their families, and contribute to the development of the community. Today about 90 percent of the people living in the Har Bracha settlement are either graduates of the yeshiva or were friends or relatives of the graduates, who decided that God wanted them in this community.

Now the whole community is built around the yeshiva and the rabbi. In other words, the Torah is the center of life in this community. Currently there are many rabbis who live in the community and teach in the growing yeshiva. The residents donate ten percent or more to support the yeshiva and keep it growing and developing. A beautiful new dining room and kitchen has been recently completed.

There are now more people who want to live in the community than there is housing, so the rabbi suggested – because of the building freeze – that all who could afford it should build a second story on their homes. This has now happened, and many families are renting out their upstairs apartments to new couples and students coming to live in the community.

The yeshiva itself is so well known that students come from all over Israel. These youth do not just study; many of them also run programs for the children and teach the Bible to them. Also, Rabbi Melamed started a program called "Combined." This program allows students who are not going to become rabbis to attend Ariel University or other colleges in the daytime, but then they return to the settlement in the evening for more Bible study. There is also a similar program for girls. About 120 young men are in the full yeshiva Bible program, and another 100 are in the Combined program, so altogether more than 200 are studying the scriptures and commentaries. Rabbi Melamed chose a key verse of Scripture as a focus and theme for all the people of this settlement, "In all your ways know God." It is read in the synagogue and posted to remind people.

One of the residents, Nir Lavi, operates a successful winery in the Har Bracha settlement. He planted vineyards, starting in 1998 that led to the first harvest in 2002. Even to this very day he is adding more and more vineyards with the help of heavy equipment used to move the rocks and smooth out the land. He is excited to be developing the land that he knows was given to Abraham, Isaac, and Jacob to help bring out the seven blessed fruits of the land, one of which is grapes, after 2,000 years of

*Har Bracha synagogue.*

*Har Bracha homes.*

no Jewish farming in this area. He feels that he is fulfilling the prophecy that says that grapes will be planted again on the hills of Samaria.

> Again you will plant vineyards on the hills of Samaria; the farmers will plant them and enjoy their fruit.
>
> (Jeremiah 31:5)

Yonatan, a tour guide who has lived in this settlement for 25 years, noted that from the settlement of Har Bracha one can see beyond the other settlements to the east, all the way to Jordan when the weather permits, because it is 2,887 feet above sea level. Yonatan is a Zionist and has been an idealist from the time he was a youth in the U.S.

The community is made up of schools, businesses, a grocery store, a post office, and two synagogues. The largest synagogue is Ashkenazi while the smaller one is Sephardic, for the Moroccans and Yemenite Jews in the community. With the encouragement of the rabbi many homes have solar panels installed, to help with power. The community is now building five new buildings that will provide 50 new apartments for students to live in.

Each year the community has to build more kindergartens and day centers because so many new people with children are coming there to live. There are now about ten kindergartens in various locations and child care centers for younger children. They are receiving help from the government, from the Settlement Council, and additional funds for their building projects from organizations such as Christian Friends of Israeli Communities. Because there is so much building going on and not enough Jewish construction workers in the area, they hire Arabs to do most of the building.

## Settlement of Rechelim

After learning about a small winery business in the settlement of Rechelim, I made several visits there. The settlement was started in 1991, and along with its neighboring settlement of Nofei Nehemiah was officially recognized by the Israeli government in 2012 as an authorized settlement. It is located just east of Ariel and adjacent to two Arab villages, Yatma and Qabalan. Even though it is a small community of only 35 families, they have a synagogue, lovely parks, a kindergarten, childcare, and a winery.

The story about what motivated people to start this settlement is an example of what motivated the beginnings of many of the settlements. On October 27, 1991, busloads of Jewish settlers were on their way to a protest rally in Tel Aviv against the peace negotiations in Madrid, when one of the buses came under attack by Palestinians. The driver, Yitzhak Rofeh, from West Jerusalem, and Rachel Drouk of Shiloh were killed. After Rachel's funeral, women from settlements all over Judea and Samaria set up tents at the site and remained there, despite government disapproval. It was named "Rechelim" (plural of the name "Rachel") after Rachel Drouk, Rachel Weiss, who was killed in a Palestinian attack in 1988, and the matriarch Rachel.

During my interview with Vered Ben Saadon, the wife of the founder of the Tura Winery I learned that her husband, Erez

Ben Saadon, established the winery in 2003 as Erez Winery and renamed it in 2005 as the Tura Winery. The grapes for their wine are grown in vineyards on Har Bracha (Mount Gerizim) at an elevation of 840 meters. In 2010, the winery was producing some 12,000 bottles annually, chiefly from Cabernet Sauvignon, Merlot and Chardonnay grapes.

It is wonderful for such a small community to have such a quality enterprise. The grapes for the winery come from some of the best vineyards in Israel, which were planted by the owners, Erez and Vered Ben Saadon, in 1997. They pride themselves on the quality of their wine because of the time they allow it to age, in perfect conditions for storage and aging. They will not sell their wine until it has sat in the barrels for two years and then another year in bottles.

To date, they have won many awards in Israel for their wines. For example, in 2012 they walked away with the Oscar Award for wine in Israel's annual Golden Grape competition for the highest quality of wine. The competition from seven other wineries in Samaria, and 63 of the finest additional wineries in all of Israel, proves even more the success of this couple and their small winery in a settlement in Samaria. They feel that they can compete because their wine is rather unique compared to others, and it is wine from the biblical mountain of blessing, Mount Gerizim.

According to Vered, the two reasons for their success is that Erez is very strict and detailed as to how the wine is made and aged, and the other reason is that they really believe that God is blessing them ... and they thank God for His favor. They now produce 14,000 bottles of wine a year. They are now exporting their 2009 wine to France, the United States, and other parts of Europe in spite of those who attempt to boycott products from the West Bank for political reasons.

They are also producing olive oil from their groves of olive trees, and a new organic apple cider beer from apple trees on Mount Gerizim. They have made their winery into a visitors center, attracting many people who come from all over Israel to

*Tura Winery wine cellar.*

enjoy the 40-minute tour and to taste and purchase wine and the other products. This is more evidence of how God is blessing the return of the Jews to the land of their biblical ancestors.

## The Settlement of Hinanit

The settlement of Hinanit is in the far northern part of Samaria. To get there it is necessary to drive west to the coastal plain before going north, and then east to Hinanit. The Palestinians and the Israeli government will no longer allow Jews to drive straight north through Samaria to the Galilee, or places such as Hinanit, even though that would be by far the shortest route. The reason for this restriction is that there are three administrative areas in Judea and Samaria. The road to Hinanit and that area unfortunately goes through Area A in which only Palestinians are allowed to live and travel. Area B is also Palestinian, but has joint Palestinian and Israel security so that both Jews and Arabs are allowed to drive in that area. However, even in Area C, which is for Jewish settlers and has only Israeli security, some Arab villages do exist in this area. Only Area A

*Hinanit administration office.*

restricts Jews totally, but Jews would not choose to drive those areas because they would be more dangerous.

Hinanit is one of seven Jewish settlements in that vicinity and one of three that are in quite close proximity to each other. These are Tal Menashe, Shaked, and Hinanit, all located on Mount Amir in the hills of Samaria. The settlement of Tal Menashe, the only religious settlement in the northern part of Samaria, was started in 1999 and is named after the tribe of Manasseh. The settlement of Shaked, meaning almond, is a secular settlement started in 1981, and in 2012, had grown to a population of about 600.

Although I have never visited the settlements of Tal Menashe or Shaked, I have visited Hinanit two times. The first time I was there, in 2011, I interviewed the leader of the community, Hanan Niv, who is the head of the council and the director of the unique immigration and Hebrew language program (ulpan) for new Russian immigrants to Israel.

He told me about how this settlement was started in 1981, mainly by mountain Jews from the Caucasus area of Russia. Hinanit is a very pleasant place for new immigrants to stay initially, as a group, to adjust to life in Israel and to learn Hebrew. Each year about 100 immigrants from Russia and Ukraine come to live and study Hebrew. Mr. Niv himself migrated with his parents to Israel, from the Caucasus in 1974, when he was only 14. He then moved to Hinanit just a year after it started when there were only 10 families living there.

The residents recently opened a new community center and have plans for more housing, schools, and a swimming pool. They have also started some industry for providing work. They have wonderful parks and a unique indoor play area for children. Because they help their Arab neighbors with water and electricity, they enjoy a positive relationship with their neighboring Arab villages. Hanan said that, because they know they will be living with their Arab neighbors for a long time, they want to cooperate with them and work together.

## The Settlement of Tzofim

The settlement of Tzofim, established in 1989, is just across the Green Line so that some would say it is on disputed land. It was started by a nucleus of 12 families who first came and lived in mobile homes, as was the case with the beginning of most of the settlements. One of Charlotte's lecturers, the wife of the rabbi in Tzofim, arranged for us to visit this settlement in March 2010. We drove about 30 minutes west to get to the area of Tzofim that includes the settlement of Alfei Menashe, Kfar Saba, and the Arab village of Qalqilya.

Since Tzofim was established, it has grown into a community of more than 1,000 residents, or about 300 separate family homes with a mixture of religious and secular. As is the case with other settlements, Tzofim has permanent homes, paved roads, nurseries, kindergartens, stores, and a synagogue. There are no schools, but the children have transportation to schools only about a 10-minute drive from Tzofim. Tzofim is also growing with many additional homes being built.

Aaron, the head of security for Tzofim, drove us to the highest part of the community where we could see the towns of Tel Aviv,

Netanya, and Hadera on the Mediterranean coast to the west of Tzofim, and also one of Israel's power plants for electricity. He pointed out that if Palestinian terrorists were to control the land of the higher elevation, like that of Tzofim, they would be able to easily fire rockets on major population centers and industrial areas along Israel's coast.

Aaron took us to their administration office where he showed us the community plans for growth, but as of then they were still waiting for permission from the Israeli government to expand the way they want to. More housing is urgently needed because there is a waiting list of people who would like to live there.

I interviewed Josh, one of the long-term residents of the community, who has lived in Tzofim for 20 years. He came to Israel from Chicago with his late wife, who came from New York. They were both raised as Orthodox Jews who belonged to a Zionist youth movement that promoted making aliyah to Israel. It seemed quite natural for them, as a family, to move to Israel, which they did in 1989.

They chose to make Tzofim their home because, while they were temporarily living in the Absorption Center after arriving in Israel on aliyah, some folks from Tzofim came and made a presentation about the community. So, just four years after Tzofim started, they bought a new home and settled into the community. It fit what they were looking for – a new settlement and a way to help develop the country of Israel. By that time people were no longer living in mobile homes but were in permanent homes. It has been a wonderful, peaceful experience for them; they have been an integral part of the community and have lots of friends.

Since Josh has lived in the community there has been very little struggle with the government, and in contrast with what happens in other settlements, each family here legally owns their own land once it has been purchased by them. It is registered in their name and is not part of a 99-year lease, or something similar. Also, at some point, even though the community is technically on Samaria land, the fence has been moved so that they are actually on the pre-Six-Day War side of Israel.

The community has recently completed the construction of the synagogue (Beit Knesset) building. There are three different synagogues for three different types of prayer services – one for the Ashkenazis, one for the Sephardis, and one for the Yemenites. The Ashkenazi synagogue is the largest of the three.

Samaria still has settlements starting up, but not without a struggle. As I have stated previously, there are Jewish settlements now spotted all over the land that was promised to Abraham, Isaac, and Jacob and their descendants. Notice that if only Abraham were mentioned, the Arabs might have a case for saying that the land traditionally belongs to them, but God narrowed the field by saying that the land was only for the descendants of Jacob.

There is so much more that I could have written but I trust that this sample about life in the Jewish settlements of Samaria will help you to appreciate what has happened in only about 40 years. These pioneers of faith need all the love and encouragement and support that you can possibly offer them. In the concluding chapter of this book I will recommend some places for you to visit and things that will help you to get involved.

I trust that this description of some the communities in Samaria and what their life is like will help you to appreciate them and to do all that you can to encourage and support them.

# 7

# Places to Visit in Samaria

In the previous six chapters I have been sharing my thoughts on the history of life in Samaria. Now, in this last chapter I want to share some information with you about some of the places you could and should visit in Samaria and the surrounding area. I will also include some of my own personal experiences while visiting these sites.

## A Bus Ride

Ideally you will be able to arrange for a guided tour of Judea and Samaria while you are visiting Israel. That is the best way to see everything and to learn as much as possible. Some folks will rent a car and find their own way around, but a safer and more efficient use of your time includes having a guide. I will list some guides in the appendix.

If your time and money are limited, then I suggest that you take the Egged bus ride from Jerusalem to Ariel, and back again. Take bus 148 from the central bus station in Jerusalem. The one-way fare is only about four U.S. dollars – you'll see so much for your money. The route varies, but it can include stops at the following settlements: Ofra, Shiloh, Eli, Ma'ale Levona, Tapuach, and Ariel.

Since bus 148 operates between Jerusalem and Ariel about 16 times a day, you can spend some time in Ariel or other stops and still make it back to Jerusalem the same day. If you stop in Ariel you could visit the Holocaust Museum or the University. Or, you could just walk the streets to sense the atmosphere and enjoy some lunch or yogurt in the shopping center of town. Usually, on the ride back to Jerusalem the bus will make some stops in Ma'ale Levona. This is quite an experience because this beautiful community is located on the very top of a fairly high mountain ridge. You will be amazed at the road that was constructed up to the settlement. This bus ride will give you an overview of Samaria that is well worth your time and money.

## Ancient Tel Shiloh

Shiloh is well worth visiting. It is a major biblical site because it is where Joshua placed the wilderness Tabernacle built by the Israelites and carried in the wilderness before the children of Israel went into the land of Canaan under Joshua. The Tabernacle in Shiloh remained there for 369 years as the religious center for all of Israel.

With a new visitors center[1] in modern Shiloh, and guided tours, it is breathtaking to see the ancient walls, cisterns, and the area where the Tabernacle stood. The location is just off Highway 60, the Highway of the Patriarchs, south of Ariel and only 27 miles north of Jerusalem.

The first time Charlotte and I visited Tel Shiloh in 2004, I was astounded to think that I was actually standing at the spot of the

*Tabernacle site at Tel Shiloh.*

[1]See the website www.telshilo.org.il.

*Shiloh ancient crafts exhibit.*

entrance to the wilderness Tabernacle. I could almost hear the voice of the High Priest Eli saying to Hannah, "Go in peace, and may the God of Israel grant you what you have asked of Him" (1 Samuel 1:17). He said this to Hannah who was asking God for a child. As you may know, that child was the Prophet Samuel.

Since then I have visited several times, and one time that stands out in my memory is a tour led by Eliana Passentin, who lives in the settlement of Eli, high on a hill overlooking ancient Tel Shiloh. When the land for her house was being cleared, pieces of broken pottery were uncovered. Since Eliana was doing graduate studies in Archeology at the time, she had some of the pieces analyzed. The scientist was quite surprised to find that the pottery dated back to the time of Joshua and the prophet Samuel. He concluded that the Israelites sat on the ground above the Tabernacle during the Jewish feasts, watching the activities and socializing. It was a requirement that any pottery used for food or water during those sacred feasts would be broken and not used again.

## Mount Gerizim

If and when you visit Tel Shiloh, on your own or with a guide, continue on Highway 60, the Highway of the Patriarchs, past Tapuach Junction and the intersection of Shechem/Nablus to the north, Har Bracha to the west, and Itamar and Elon Moreh to the east. You will turn left at that traffic circle and drive up the hill, past the entrance to the settlement of Har Bracha and on to the Samaritan village. You will then drive through the Samaritan village and on to a high point on Mount Gerizim (Har Bracha/ Mountain of Blessing), mentioned several times in the Bible and in this book.

This high point provides a marvelous view of the area. When you look to the east you will see Mount Kabir, which many believe is the mountain on which Abraham stood to first view the Land after arriving. As you look slightly north and down on the Arab town of Shechem/Nablus, your guide can point out the location of Joseph's Tomb. Jews are not allowed into the city except once

*Samaritan temple ruins.*

*Samaritan museum and priest.*

a month, at night, to visit Joseph's Tomb, but if you are a tourist with the right guide you may be allowed to visit Nablus and Joseph's Tomb. If you are not able to visit Shechem, the view from Mount Gerizim is the closest you can get to Joseph's Tomb.

I cannot count the number of times that I have visited Mount Gerizim, but each time has been very special and each time the weather has been different. I would also suggest that you do not leave that area without visiting the Samaritan museum in the Samaritan village, Kiryat Luza, that you pass through on the way to the lookout on Mount Gerizim. Either your tour guide or you can arrange for the Samaritan high priest to open the museum and guide you through. His explanation is well worth your time. Also, you might have time for the short walk to the ruins of the fortified church and the remains of the Samaritan temple.

I would also recommend that you visit the local Tahini factory while you are in Kiryat Luza. Here you can see the whole process of crushing the hulled sesame seeds from Ethiopia and producing bottles of Sesame Tahinim which is used in many Middle Eastern

*Hiking on Mount Kabir.*

dishes, and it is very healthy. This is one of the first industries started by the Samaritans. While in the factory they will offer you a small sample to taste. It is so unique and delicious with such a pleasant smell. It is delicious on salads and other foods. Anyone in the village can direct you to it.

Hopefully you will also have time to visit the Jewish community of Har Bracha. It is best if you have a guide for that because he will need to let the folks there know ahead of time.

Once you descend from Mount Gerizim back down to Highway 60, continue east toward the settlement of Elon Moreh. You will drive through Elon Moreh to Mount Kabir. It is possible to drive up Mount Kabir quite a ways before you park and walk an easy trail around the summit that includes some spectacular views of the Mevo HaShemesh Road, which is known as the Entrance to Sun Highway traveled by the patriarchs. Also to the north is the spectacular view of the Valley of Tirzah. As you view much of Israel from there, you will be reminded of all that Abraham could see and marvel at, just after he first entered the Land.

## Joshua's Altar

Mount Kabir also affords a great view of both Mount Gerizim and Mount Ebal (Mount of Blessings and Mount of Curses). If you have a guide, he will be able to point out the location of Joshua's altar on Mount Ebal, which is mentioned in the Book of Joshua. Unfortunately, it is hard to visit Joshua's altar, but it is open certain times of the year during Jewish holidays. I have never been fortunate enough to visit there yet.

## Sebastia

I was able to visit Sebastia, known as Samaria in the Bible and is the ruins of the capital built by King Omri.

Samaria is the name of the capital of the ten northern tribes, known in the Bible as Israel, in contrast to Jerusalem, the capital of the southern tribes known in the Bible as Judea.

When you visit Sebastia you will see the remains of terraces built by the Israelites 3,000 years ago. In the first century BCE, King Herod rebuilt Sebastia as a Roman metropolis and then changed the name to Sebaste in honor of Roman Emperor Augustus. Because of its location, a person or tour guide needs to arrange with the Israel Defense Force to visit the area.

My guess is that there may be a way for a non-Jewish tourist to visit this national park if they make arrangements with an Arab tour company. In fact, it might be possible to visit other sites off limits to Jews if you are not Jewish by contacting an Arab tour company or by taking a bus directly from Ramallah or East Jerusalem. Once you are in Nablus you can walk to most of the sites. There are several sites of interest. However, I would recommend that you use a tour guide and not try it on your own.

## Elon Moreh

As mentioned earlier, while you are in Elon Moreh you will

find it very interesting to tour the factory that prepares animal skins to be written on by scribes for the Torah. It is an interesting process that a guide can explain to you. I have arranged for several individuals to tour the factory. Your guide can also arrange for you to visit a scribe in Elon Moreh, and watch him write the Hebrew letters on animal skin. This is a rich experience because it is something that has been done this way for thousands of years.

I suggest that on the way back to Highway 60 you visit the Itamar area. A guide can show you around and explain the history and life of the community. I have visited this area many times, and each time has been extremely rewarding. Here are some of the things that I would strongly recommend: Gideon's Tomb, Three Seas Observation Point (on a clear day you can see the Mediterranean Sea, Sea of Galilee, and the Dead Sea), and Givat Olam Organic Farm. You will really enjoy the animals, fresh organic yogurt, and more. Before you leave Itamar, hopefully you will visit the Zimmerman Farm and taste some of their delicious food items.

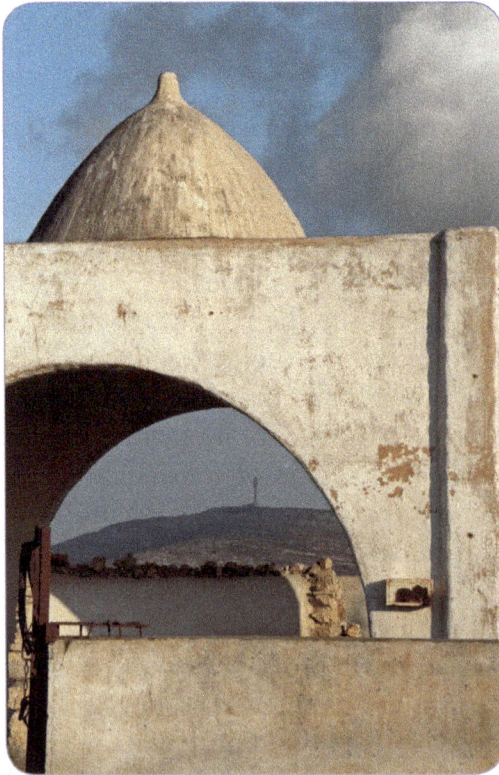

*Gideon's Tomb.*

## Kedumim – Kedem Museum

Don't miss a visit to the Kedem Museum in Kedumim on Highway 55, which runs east and west to Highway 60, a little north of Ariel. This little-known museum is a treasure that displays items that were excavated in Kedumim as the settlement developed. The initial discoveries were made when building began in the seventies. I suppose you could say that this in itself is one of the unexpected benefits of Jewish settlement in Samaria.

Initially an Israeli army officer in charge of archaeology noticed some things uncovered accidently during construction. Some ceramic findings in graves show that the area was first settled 5,000 years ago during the Bronze Age. British scientists did some digging in this area in the 1800s, and then American Rabbi Nelson Glueck did some more work in the 1930s. Kedumim was the first dig, and further research of the rural portions of Samaria revealed much about the history of common life in the area.

Museum displays show the following ages: Pre-Historical age, Chalcolithic age, Early Bronze, Middle Bronze, Period of the Patriarchs, Tel Shiloh, Iron Age, Samaritans, Beginning Persian, Persian and Hellenistic, and Roman and Byzantine. Also on display is an ancient olive press, reconstructed grave, sun dials, stone tools, and mosaic wall. It is best to make an appointment ahead of time. A tour guide in Samaria can make those arrangements for you.

*Kedem Museum.*

## Ariel

I hope your visit includes Ariel, the largest community in Samaria. There are ancient ruins that have been discovered on the outskirts of the town.

In a village just outside of Ariel to the west is the burial place of Joshua. Because of its location in an Arab village, Jews and others are allowed to visit the site only at certain times of the year.

Also on the westerly side of Ariel is the Eshel HaShomron Hotel. Even if you do not stay in hotel, it is well worth a visit because of their Garden of Biblical Samaria, which will bring much of the Bible to life for you. You will see breathtaking Bible paintings that fill the whole wall of a large room. [2]

Ariel is the home of a very unique Holocaust Museum. I am sad to report that just before this book went to press I learned of the passing of Yaakov Wodislavsky, a survivor of the Holocaust who owned and operated the museum. Known to many as Kuba, he would give a talk at the end of the tour, answer questions, and show a movie. He is survived by his wife, Irena. I hope that Irena will be able to keep the doors to this special museum open.

*Kuba and Irena, Ariel Holocaust Museum.*

If there is time, be sure to include a tour of Ariel University.

## Other Areas in Judea and Samaria To Visit

Other areas to include in your visits to Judea and Samaria are as follows: Ancient Hebron (burial place of the Patriarchs

---

[2]The hotel's web address: http://www.eshelhashomron.com

Abraham, Isaac, and Jacob), Prat Spring Reserve (the Prophet Jeremiah's home area), the Binyamin Presentation and Wine Tasting Visitors Center, Genesis Land (step back 4,000 years to ride a camel to Abraham's tent for lunch with Abraham himself), The Good Samaritan Inn (the only mosaic museum in Israel), and Beit El (Bethel in the Bible). You can also tour the area where the rock that Jacob slept on is located, and Gush Etzion, starting with the ancient remains from the Second Temple period and including the moving sound and light show portraying Gush Etzion's creation, fall, and eventual renewal, plus the breathtaking views in modern Gush Etzion.

## Conclusion

Most tour guides overlook many of the areas that I have mentioned in this chapter. This is such a shame because Judea and Samaria are the areas where most of the events in the Bible took place. This is what is called the biblical heartland of Israel. Much of the travel information makes the security problems of Judea and Samaria seem much worse than it really is. After all, any place in the world can be dangerous under certain circumstances.

Recently someone coined the term "The Bible Belt of Israel." This area contains the greatest concentration of Jews in the world, most with a strong faith in Abraham, Isaac, and Jacob. This is the area that is coming alive in preparation for the Messiah. Visiting Israel will be a rich experience, but it will be even richer if you include visiting Judea and Samaria.

I want to encourage you to include this area in your visit. The first time I visited this area was in 2004, and my life has never been the same.

## Appendix A

## Tours and Guides for Judea and Samaria

Love Israel Tours
loveisraeltours@aol.com       US Phone: 904-638-5397

Gershon Portnoy
tour@gershontg.com       IL Phone: 972-2-997-3676

Eliana Passentin
eli@hadar-yosef.org.il       IL Phone: 972-2-940-0148

David Ha'ivri
haivri@yeshuv.org       IL Phone: 972-3-936-8146

Yair Shalev
yshalev@gmail.com       IL Phone: 972-52-349-2217

Special tours are conducted in Samaria during the Jewish high holidays.

Two 1-Day Tours in biblical Israel by Christian Friends of Israeli Communities. Phone: US: 719-683-2014 / 800-647-3344 or Israel 972-9-792-0958. Email: sondra@cfoic.com.

Nine-day tour by Ovadyah Avrahami of KOL HATOR. For details – http://www.shomron-samaria.com/Tours.html#SuccotTour

## Information, Funding Projects, and Volunteering

Shomron Liaison Office
www.goshomron.com                    IL Phone: 972-3-936-8146

Shiloh Israel Children's Fund
www.shilohisraelchildren.org         US Phone: 877-742-2064

Christian Friends of Israeli Communities
www.cfoic.com                        US Phone: 800-647-3344

Hayovel
(Volunteers who help Jews pruning and harvesting grapes)
http://www.hayovel.com

## Videos of Samaria

http://www.youtube.com/watch?v=kWZNNWGY7V0

http://www.youtube.com/watch?v=11Hri4fdwf8

http://www.youtube.com/watch?v=EENjik-yeec

http://www.youtube.com/watch?v=7Fi72dEA-NI

http://www.youtube.com/watch?v=hSUkMFAqllI

http://www.youtube.com/watch?feature=player_embedded&v=-YF0YzhGDdk#!

http://www.youtube.com/watch?feature=player_embedded&v=tGZHlKapdmE

http://www.youtube.com/watch?v=pek724l53PI

http://www.youtube.com/watch?v=Vk1AhMcWp1E

## Appendix B
# Ten Reasons

By Ezra Ridgley

1.  **Need for Security.** We already have 21 Arab nations and so why add another. If the 22$^{nd}$ state is established it would reduce Israel at the narrowest part to a nine mile strip. 350 million Arabs who have an ideology to destroy the Jews and Israel already surround Israel. There is no way that this is going to bring peace. Land for peace has never worked and it will never work.

2.  **Desecration of God's Name.** The Jews are the torch bearer of the Torah to the rest of the world. God set the Jews as an example of those who follow God to the rest of the world. If the Jews give away the Land, it shows the world that they no longer believe in the law and the promises of God that they have held to for 4000 years during both the time of the Temple and during the years of prayer. This would be a desecration of God's name at the highest level. Can you imagine the people of God who are supposed to show the world what faith in God is, give up on their faith? The land is a vital part of the Jewish Faith. The Jews must not substitute their faith in God for faith in the US, EU, or UN.

3.  **Destruction of the Jewish Identity.** So much of the Jewish identity is connected with the land of Israel and especially Judea and Samaria. The land is where the Torah took place and this land was promised to the Father of faith, Abraham. If the Jews were to give this land up, it would be like destroying all of those promises made to Abraham and destroy us as a people and destroying the Jewish soul. The purpose of the Jewish existence and has kept the Jewish people alive all these years with the hope of returning.

How can they now say that this land has no meaning after praying and waiting to return to the land for 2000 years. It would destroy everything that we believe in as a people.

4. **Legally it is our Land.** Today, according to present day international law, Israel including Judea and Samaria and Jerusalem legally belong to the Jews, but the leaders and international powers never talk about it. The mandate of Palestine in 1922 states that recognition is given to the historical connection between the Jewish people and Palestine and for grounds for reinstituting a national homeland for the Jewish people in that country. Judea and Samaria is the center of that homeland and historically it was the first area of Israel/Palestine to be settled after the Jews entered the land. This mandate was adopted by the League of Nations and fully adopted in charter 80 by the UN and has never been superseded by any law at any time since. Even the Partition Plan of 1947 was a General Assembly resolution non-binding and it was rejected by the Arabs. Besides this the 2012 Levi report by retired Supreme Court Justice, Edmond Levy, concluded that Israel's presence in the West Bank is not occupation and that the Jewish settlements are legal under international law and recommends state approval for all unauthorized outposts.

5. **Historically it is Jewish Land.** Since the historical time of Joshua conquering the land no other race of people have ever settled in Israel, but instead there were only foreign occupying powers were present when the Jews were not ruling there. Even during the last 2000 years the Jews have always been there to some degree. A census by the British embassy in 1864 found that 80% of the population of Jerusalem was Jewish. There have always been some Jews in the land. But for much of that time the land was desolate. It was so desolate and desert-like that the Muslims and Arabs did not want to live in it. Starting in the 1800s the Jews started draining the swamps and renewing the land

into an agricultural paradise. Arabs would travel through the area, but very few settled down and there was never any large population group of Arabs in the land. Many more Arabs came for work after the Jews returned and started turning the desert green.

6. **Religiously it is the Jewish Land.** God gave the land to the Jews as a covenant. It is a sign of the promises that God made with Abraham while he was in Samaria – "To you and your descendants I will give this land." The Jews hold on to the fact that the promises will be fulfilled. Any rights that Muslims or Christians would give as to why they might have a right to the land are traced back to a great Jewish nation. Christians and Muslims received their faith in God because of a great Jewish nation that once lived on this land. Therefore it is the Jews only who have a religious right to the land. How can the others say that because they have faith in God they have a right to the land?

7. **Morally it is the Jewish Land.** The Palestinians are trying to acquire the land through the shedding of innocent blood for over a hundred years. The land for peace is an extortion attempt. Extortion is obtaining the property of another induced by wrongful use of actual or threatened force, violence, or fear, or under color of official right. This outlines essentially what the entire land for peace process is. Anyone who is helping with this either consciously or unconsciously is a co-extortionist because they are helping the extortionist acquire their property through the most vile and evil means. One needs to understand that land for peace is an extortion attempt to take land that belongs to the Jews through violence, death, and all kinds of things.

8. **Tikun Olam – The restoration of the world.** The entire deliverance and peace for mankind rests on the shoulders of the Jewish people. If Israel can't rebuild their nation and *shalom* does not come over Israel, then *shalom* cannot come over mankind because the Jews are the head of the

nations. If the head is sick, the whole body is sick. The head is where all the knowledge, intelligence, ideas, and inspiration come from and that is Israel. Even in the midst of difficulties, Israel is showing that kind of leadership. It is in the interest of the entire world that they support Israel in building the greatest nation on earth and to bring peace to Israel. God has said, "My house is a house of prayer for all nations." Peace has to come to Israel before it comes to the rest of the world and so when they make war against Israel they are really making war against themselves. He who curses Israel will be cursed and he who blesses Israel will be blessed. For example, Israel has more charity organizations per capita than any other country. Israel has less murders than any other country; and less than Toronto, known to be the safest city in North America. Israel shines in technology, bringing things like the computer chip to the rest of the world, and too much more to mention here. Israel is the light to rest of the world spiritually and in technology, advancement, civil order, and much more. The more other countries support Israel, the more they will benefit from all that Israel has to offer.

9. **Land for Future Generations**. The Jews still need a place to live and there are still six million Jews living in North America and eight million worldwide. It is the hope that one day all Jews will be living in Israel. Our children will need a place to live and this the Jewish house and land they cannot allow anyone else to control it.

10. **A Sin Against Those who Perished in the Holocaust**. It was Arab violence during pre state years that caused the British to renege on the mandate for Palestine homeland for the Jews in 1922. In 1937, the British decided that there was a need to divide the land because of all the violence that was occurring. They restricted Jewish immigration while they opened the floodgates for Arab immigration. The White Paper of 1939 declared that there

would be no homeland for the Jews in Palestine. This meant that the Jews in Europe and Russia had nowhere to flee to in 1939 because it was not under Jewish rule, but under British rule. Millions of Jews could have been saved from the Holocaust. It was Arab violence that triggered the British to make such decisions. It would be trampling on the blood of those who died in the Holocaust if the people who contributed to their demise should inherit the land that was here waiting for them.[1]

[1]Ridgley, Ezra B. Ten Reasons. Tamar Yonah Show, Israel National Radio, 2013. http://www.youtube.com/watch?v=tOODW3QeCuM

## Appendix C
# How did the Jews get to where they are today?

| Date | |
|------|---|
| | **Historical Events of Israel** |
| Ca 2030 BCE | God promised the land of the Levant to Abraham as an inheritance in order that He could use that strategic position from which to bless the world. Abraham lived in the land alongside other immigrants and later purchased land in Hebron for burying his wife Sarah. Gen. 23:3-20 |
| Ca 1900 BCE | Isaac and Jacob grew up in the land and when he came back from the years in Haran, he moved to Shechem and purchased land there. Gen. 33:18-20 |
| 1400 BCE to 1330 BCE | Israel under Joshua's leadership entered and conquered the land of Canaan. The Canaanites were gradually decimated and the population came to be known as Phoenicians, located in what is Lebanon today. The Israelites took possession of the land as directed by God. |
| 1010 BCE to 930 BCE | King David and King Solomon ruled after the land was conquered. Habitation in the land was only disputed by the Philistines, who emigrated from the area around Crete. Solomon's kingdom included all of Israel and much of what is Jordan and Syria today. |
| 722 BCE | Assyria took Israel into captivity. They left Jews to mingle with new Gentile settlers. The resulting Samaritans have lived in part of the northern part of what is known as the West Bank until today. |

| Date | |
|------|--|
| | **Historical Events of Israel** |
| 606 BCE<br>to<br>586 BCE | Babylon destroyed the Temple and took the influential people of Judah into captivity. The poorest people were left there to work the fields. |
| 536 BCE<br>to<br>440 BCE | Jews returned to Jerusalem to rebuild the Temple and repopulate their land. They took drastic steps to purify the Jewish race. |
| 540<br>to 330 BCE | The Persian Empire had conquered Babylon so they assumed rule over the land of Israel. |
| 320 BCE<br>to 200 BCE | Alexander the Great took control, and Ptolemaic Rule ensued (Greek). |
| 200 BCE<br>to 166 BCE | Seleucid Rule – They were major proponents of Hellenistic Culture – still Greek domination. |
| 140 BCE<br>to<br>63 BCE | The Maccabean Jews revolted against the Greeks and the Jewish Hasmonean Dynasty began to rule – the only time Jews had self-rule between 610 BCE and 1948. This was known as the independent Kingdom of Israel. |
| 63 BCE<br>to<br>135 CE | Pompey of the Romans assumed control over Judea when Jewish kings were involved in a dispute over power. The Jews lived under the Romans but exercised their own religious rule through the priesthood and the Sanhedrin. In 135 AD the Jews were forbidden by the Romans to set foot in Jerusalem again. |
| 63 BCE<br>to<br>476 CE | The Roman Empire retained control over the land. The land of Canaan / the land of Israel began to be called "Palestine." Palestine came from "Philistine" used in a derogatory sense. |
| 476 CE<br>to<br>1453 | Roman Rule from the Eastern empire, centered in Constantinople. This largely coincided with the Byzantine period and lasted until the Ottoman tribe conquered Constantinople. |

| Date | |
|------|---|
| | **Historical Events of Israel** |
| 324 to 638 CE | Byzantine Period: Christian influence; Constantine's mother built churches in many places in Israel. Christian pilgrims from Europe visited Israel. |
| 638 to 1099 CE | Muslim Period: This is the first time that anyone like Arabs began to live in the land except for the Edomites, who became Jews in the two centuries before Jesus in order to be identified as legitimate inhabitants of the land. |
| 1099 to 1187 CE | Christian Crusader Period. Armies from Europe tried to free Israel from the hands of the Muslims. Many Muslims and Jews were killed. |
| 1187 to 1260 CE | Ayyubid Period – a Muslim dynasty of Kurdish origin, founded by Saladin and centered in Egypt, conquered surrounding nations and territory. Most of the Kingdom of Jerusalem fell to Saladin after his victory at the Battle of Hattin in 1187. However, the Crusaders regained control of Palestine's coastline in the 1190s. |
| 1260 to 1517 CE | Mamluk Period – a powerful Egyptian military caste ruled as sultans in the Levant. They fought the last of the Crusaders and drove them out of Palestine. |
| 1517 to 1917 CE | Ottoman Period – The Ottomans conquered Constantinople in 1453 and thus became a widespread Empire, taking over the control of the area of Palestine. From Turkey, known as Turkish Rule. |
| 1917 to 1948 CE | British Mandate period – Great Britain was given oversight over Turkish territory by the UN after the Axis powers were defeated in WWI. |
| 1948 to Present | Independent country of Israel |

| Date | |
|---|---|
| | **Recent Land Issues and Measures** |
| Late 1800s | Zionists' migration to Palestine (Israel) during Ottoman Period. At this time the Arabs were the majority living in the land but Jews had been persecuted for centuries in Europe and were eager to get back to their land. |
| Early 1900s | More Jewish migration to Palestine (Israel) during Ottoman Period. |
| 1917 | Balfour Declaration written by United Kingdom's Foreign Secretary, Arthur James Balfour, showing favor for establishing a homeland for the Jews, not a "state." He declared all of Israel and Jordan today as the place for this homeland, but there was the understanding that nothing should be done to prejudice the existing civil and religious rights of the non-Jewish communities in Palestine. |
| April 25, 1920 | San Remo Resolution signed by League of Nations established the boundaries of the Palestinian homeland for the Jews including all of Israel today, the West Bank (of the Jordan River) and the entire Sea of Galilee, Jordan River, and Dead Sea. It also included a narrow strip of southern Lebanon. This was less than that suggested by the Balfour Declaration. |
| May 1939 | The MacDonald White Paper declared that Britain did not intend for Palestine to become a Jewish State and it sought to eliminate Jewish immigration to Palestine. Britain overstepped its legal powers. The Jewish Agency hoped to persuade the British to restore Jewish immigration rights, and it cooperated with the British in the war against Fascism. Aliyah Bet was organized to spirit Jews out of Nazi controlled Europe, despite the British prohibitions. |

| Date | |
|------|--|
| | **Recent Land Issues and Measures** |
| April 1946 | The Anglo-American Committee of Inquiry approved immediate acceptance of 100,000 Jewish immigrants to Palestine and the British government asked for American troops to help maintain order against an Arab revolt. |
| November 29, 1947 | The Partition: The UN voted to end the British mandate and establish two states. One for the Jews and one for the Palestinians. It partitioned the land area of "Palestine" into motley pieces assigned to each group (Resolution 181). The Arabs were assigned most of the arable land and major aquifers.<br><br>Jews were assigned a larger portion of land, most of it in the Negev desert, which allowed room for new Jewish immigration but was unsuitable for agriculture. Much of their coastal portion was populated by an Arab majority.<br><br>Although the Jews did not appreciate the boundaries which did not give them access to the Old City of Jerusalem, they accepted the Partition Plan, because it might make the establishment of a sovereign Jewish State possible. After WWII the urgent felt need of the Jews for a homeland was extremely great.<br><br>But Ben-Gurion noted that there was no certainty that their portion of the land would remain in Jewish hands as long as only 60% of the population was Jewish. The Jewish leadership recognized that a war with the Arabs would be imminent, but they hoped that statehood would make eventual territorial expansion possible. |

| Date | |
|------|---|
| | **Recent Land Issues and Measures** |
| (cont)<br>November 29,<br>1947 | The Arabs rejected the Partition, noting that the Jews had no legal or moral basis for claims to the country and Arab people constituted 65% of the entire population at that time. They insisted that the Partition plan was unfair, and they claimed the whole of Palestine.<br><br>Arab leaders threatened the Jewish population, speaking of "driving the Jews into the sea" and ridding Palestine "of the Zionist plague." |
| May 15, 1948 | On May 14, the Jewish People's Council approved a proclamation declaring the "the establishment of a Jewish State in Israel, to be known as the State of Israel."<br><br>The UN voted for the establishment of the independent State of Israel thereby endorsing the West Bank partition rejected by the Arabs in 1947. In spite of the fact that the Arabs did not accept the Partition, the British approved the plan but took as their sole responsibility the cancelling of their Mandate and their complete withdrawal.<br><br>That very day the Arab-Israeli War began with the invasion of, or intervention in, Palestine by the Arab States. |
| May 15, 1948<br>to<br>March 10,<br>1949 | Israel had to fight a war of independence to actually occupy the land they were given. Several Arab countries attacked Israel because of the UN vote, desiring to push the Jews into the sea.<br><br>During the fighting, many Arabs fled from their homes in Israel; others were expelled. Israel was victorious in winning the land they had been assigned. Many Arabs waited on the borders as refugees. |

| Date | Recent Land Issues and Measures |
|---|---|
| (cont) May 15, 1948 to March 10, 1949 | Jordan took control of what is now called the West Bank and would eventually (in 1950) annex it into the new Kingdom of Jordan. Palestinian Arabs were initially given Jordanian citizenship, but stripped of that within a few years. Jordan has a concern about Palestinians taking over. |
| March 10, 1949 | Armistice was declared and both sides agreed on a temporary border, but not a formal border. This was called "The Green Line," and it left Israel with much less land than they hoped for because Jordan occupied the West Bank and East Jerusalem, and Syria occupied the Golan Heights. Many Arabs who did not flee the land stayed in the West Bank, but many "refugees" have never come back. The Arab countries of Jordan, Syria, and Lebanon have never instated them as citizens of their countries, and although they live in permanent communities in those countries, they are still referred to as "refugees" but technically they are not. |
| June 1967 | Syria, Egypt, and Jordan again attacked Israel. In a way this was a continuation of the war of independence, and within six days Israel regained their land they lost in 1949 – namely the West Bank, the Golan Heights, and the Sinai Peninsula. Although East Jerusalem and the Golan Heights (near Syria) were annexed, Israel did not at that time intend to officially annex the West Bank – south Judea, Samaria, and the Jordan Valley. These, however, had been won back in war and were under Israeli military control receiving back in a way what was Israel's in 1948. |

| Date | |
|------|---|
| | **Recent Land Issues and Measures** |
| 1967 | Israel gave citizenship to Arabs who live in Israeli territory. Jews begin to settle in Judea and the Jordan Valley and areas previously claimed by the Arabs. The UN, spurred on by Egypt, Jordan, Israel and Lebanon, called for Israeli withdrawal from occupied territories, but there was no Palestinian organization recognized who could be involved in the effort. |
| 1969 | Yasser Arafat from Egypt began to push for a Palestinian state. He became recognized as the leader of the "Palestinian" Arab community, the Palestinian Liberation Organization. |
| 1973 | Egypt and Syria again attacked Israel on Yom Kippur (the Day of Atonement). Israel did not lose any land but instead nearly captured Cairo, Egypt and Damascus, Syria. The Sinai Peninsula remained in Israeli hands. |
| 1973 | Jews begin to settle in Samaria and Benjamin – parts of the West Bank. This is known as the "settlement movement" to the Jews, but as "illegal settlements" to the Arabs. |
| 1979 | Israel signed a peace treaty with Egypt, brokered by Pres. Carter, as the first Camp David Accords. Israel gave up the Sinai Peninsula they captured in 1967 in order to make a peace treaty with Egypt. For many years they have had a peace treaty with both Egypt and Jordan. |
| 1988 | Although they had formally rejected the Resolution 181 plan in 1988, the Palestine Liberation Organization published the Palestinian Declaration of Independence relying on the Resolution, arguing that it continues to provide international legitimacy for the right of the Palestinian people to sovereignty and national independence. |

| Date | |
|------|--|
| | **Recent Land Issues and Measures** |
| (cont)<br>1988 | The UN International Court of Justice held that the right of self-determination under international law applies to the territory and to the Palestinian people and entitles the Palestinian people to a State of their own as originally envisaged in Resolution 181. This judgment reinforced the 1947 UN Plan of Partition that the Arabs rejected and may have strengthened the Palestinians' claim to statehood.<br><br>Until 1974, Jordan demanded the restoration of its control over the West Bank. But in 1988, Jordan ceded its claims to the West Bank to the Palestine Liberation Organization, as "the sole legitimate representative of the Palestinian people. |
| 1987-1993 | The first intifada. Palestinians from many small organizations began to protest Israel's strong-arm policies and settlement within the Green Line. They interpreted Israeli reaction to their protests and willful acts of revenge, and the violence increased. Consequently Israel reacted by killing and imprisoning many Palestinians. Fed by false rumors, the rioting, burning, and bombing by the Palestinians increased, and the world began to take notice and sympathize with the oppressed and humiliated Palestinians. UN calls for Israeli cessation of deportations and military activity, as well as official condemnations were rejected by the Israelis.<br><br>The outcome was that Arafat and the PLO grew in the eyes of the world. Israel was widely condemned by world nations and leaders for her heavy-handed response to the Palestinian provocations. Arafat decided to recognize Israel's existence and to accept a two-state solution. |

| Date | |
|------|---|
| | **Recent Land Issues and Measures** |
| 1993 | Israeli Prime Minister Rabin, USA President Clinton, and Yasser Arafat, the leader of the Palestinian Liberation Organization (PLO), signed the Oslo Accords. This created a Palestinian interim self-government, the Palestinian National Authority, to end the intifada attacks on Jews, and it gave responsibility for the administration of the West Bank to the Palestinian Authority. |
| | The Oslo Accords also called for the withdrawal of the Israel Defense Forces (IDF) from the Gaza Strip and West Bank, which call Israel rejected.. Prime Minister Rabin officially acclaimed the Palestinian Liberation Organization (PLO) as a terrorist organization, but Israel withdrew its military rule from most of the West Bank that it had recaptured in 1967. |
| 1997 | Prime Minister Netanyahu signed the Hebron Protocol. This includes the redeployment of Israeli forces from Hebron and the turnover of civilian authority in much of the West Bank area to the Palestinian Authority. The PA agreed to combat terroristic practices. |
| 2000 | The Middle East Peace Summit at Camp David with President Clinton, Yasser Arafat, and Israeli Prime Minister Ehud Barak came to no agreement. Barak offered 100% of the Gaza strip and 73% of the West Bank to Arafat and the Palestinians with promised expansion of their territory up to 91%. He also agreed to give up 63 settlements but retain some of the larger ones. But **Arafat turned this offer down.** The Palestinians demanded complete sovereignty over East Jerusalem and its holy sites. Israel refused to give up sovereignty over the Jewish holy sites that it controlled. Neither side would budge on the control of the Temple Mount in Jerusalem. |

| Date | |
|------|--|
| | **Recent Land Issues and Measures** |
| (cont) 2000 | Another issue – the "Right of Return": in the 1948 war, about 500,000 Arabs had fled their homes in the land. Their descendants number about 4 million now, and the Palestinians are demanding the right to return to their property or to receive adequate compensation. The Israelis cannot offer this privilege because the sheer numbers of Arabs would overwhelm their state. They argue that many more Jews have been expelled from Arab countries since 1948 and have never been compensated or given refugee status. It was for those Jews that the state of Israel was formed. Israel did offer to absorb 100,000 so-called refugees and would contribute to the others' resettlement or absorption in other countries or the Palestinian state. |
| | The failure of the Peace Summit has largely been blamed on Arafat's commitment to a 'one-state solution' and his refusal to accept the offer without the promise of the right of return for displaced Arabs and their descendants. |
| 2000 to 2005 | The second intifada began, marked by many Palestinian suicide bombers inflicting casualties on Jewish population and Israeli retaliation and further killing. This forced the Israelis to build a wall separating the major Palestinian villages from the Israeli territory. The barrier essentially followed the "Green Line" but it caused Palestinians the hardship of not being able to work in Israel, and the Israeli government has demolished Israeli houses and settlement on the east side of the wall. |

| Date | |
|------|---|
| | **Recent Land Issues and Measures** |
| 2005 | In a bid to exchange "land for peace," Prime Minister Ariel Sharon pulled all of the Jews out of the Gaza strip ("disengagement"), but there has been no ensuing peace, instead thousands of rockets fired into Israel. |
| 2007 | Hamas, the terrorist wing of the Palestinian Authority, won the Palestinian election and assumed primacy in Gaza. As the government in charge, who would be expected to provide healthcare, utilities, and education for their people, Hamas' sole objective seems to be to rid the land of Jews. |
| | The Israelis have consistently supplied water, electricity, and medical services to the Gaza strip. However, members of Hamas have barraged southern towns in Israel with rocket fire for several years, terrorizing Israeli citizens. Hamas has stored its munitions and actually launched its bombs from schoolyards, hospitals, and civilian neighborhoods, so twice in self-defense Israel has felt forced to retaliate with air strikes in an attempt to knock out Hamas munitions. Collateral damage has been sustained, including the killing of some Palestinian civilians. Much of the world seems to see Israel as being at fault, but some recent rhetoric has granted Israel the right to defend itself. |
| November 2012 | UN voted to recognize Palestine as a non-member observer state, a new sovereign nation that has never before existed in the annals of history: Palestinian leaders have refrained from ever acknowledging Israel's right to exist at all. |

# Summary of current situation in Judea and Samaria

Since the Oslo Accords, as part of the interim Palestinian Authority the area of Judea and Samaria has been divided into three sections, sprinkled about the country:

- Section A is to be completely under the control of the Palestinian security forces. The heaviest Arab population is in cities like Nablus (Shechem), Ramallah, Bethlehem, and Hebron. The Palestinian Authority is located mainly in Ramallah, headed by Abbas. Ramallah, the government seat of the PA, and Nablus are also in section A and completely under the PA.

- Section B sports shared control by both the Palestinian security forces and the Israel Defense Force. Jericho would be an example of this. It is in a clearly defined Palestinian area, but Israelis patrol the area. Hebron is mostly under the PA, but there are still Israel Defense Forces present there especially at the Tomb of Patriarchs. For this reason many tourists still visit there.

- Section C is completely under the Israel Defense Force. (West) Jerusalem is an Israeli city.

In between these cities are both Jewish communities and smaller Arab villages. If it were to be all turned over to the PA then that would require a much larger disengagement than that of Gaza.

The colored sections on a West Bank map make the area look Swiss cheese with Palestinian villages interspersed with Israeli settlements. At this stage there are no clear boundaries. Today there are Jews and Arabs working together, Arabs working for Jews and Jews working under Arabs. Jews frequent Arab businesses in the West Bank, and Arabs are much better off financially than Arabs in the countries around Israel.

The PLO hoped that gradually they would take control of more of the area, but this has not happened. Many Jews feel that they have they right to live in the land of their ancestors because of Biblical history and the promise of God to give that land to the children of Israel. For this reason the number of settlements is growing, but they are taking land that they have legally purchased from Arabs, a normal transaction in most countries.

However, from ancient times, several countries have conquered the inhabitants of this land in wars – the Greeks, the Romans, the Muslims, the Crusaders, the Egyptians, the Turks, and now the Israelis. Much of the reality of the Jewish claim to the land can be traced to the 1948 and 1967 wars, in addition to the Biblical mandate and the UN's assignment of land to them. However the Palestinians feel that their heavy presence in the land for recent centuries gives them just cause to reject the claims whether by conquering the land or by being endowed with land and rights.

Meanwhile this "Heartland of Israel" has important places for Christians and Jews to cherish and to visit, including the Tomb of the Patriarchs, Shiloh, where Joshua placed the Tabernacle for 369 years, Gideon's Tomb, Mount Kabir (Abraham's mountain), Joseph's Tomb, Joshua's Tomb, Joshua's Altar, Mount Gerizim (Mount of Blessing), and Jacob's well.

Kathleen Bruce and Frank Mecklenburg
November 30, 2012

# Bibliography

Benzimra, Salomon. *The Jewish People's Rights to the Land of Israel*. CILR. Kindle. Copyright 2011.

Grief, Howard. *The Legal Foundation and Borders of Israel under International Law*. Jerusalem: Mazo Publishers Kindle Edition, 2010.

Nisan, Mordechai (2011-06-29). *Only Israel West of the River: The Jewish State & the Palestinian Question* (p. 50). Kindle Edition.

Oren, Michael B. Six *Days of War*. New York, NY: Random House Ballantine Publishing Group, 2002, 2003.

Peters, Joan. *From Time Immemorial*. Chicago, IL: J. KAP Publications, 1984.

Rabinovich, Abraham. *The Yom Kippur War*. New York: Schocken Books, 2003.

Ridgley, Ezra. *Judea and Samaria The Land of God*. USA: House of David Publishing, 2012.

Rubin, David. *Peace for Peace*. Israel: Shiloh Israel Press, 2013.

Safran, Nadav. *From War To War*. New York: Pegasus, 1969.

Sharon, Ariel. *Warrior*. New York: Simon & Schuster, 1989.

# Credits

## Maps courtesy of the Yesha Council
Pages 26, 29, 32, 38, 53, 56.

## Photos by Ted Mecklenburg
Pages 87, 107, 112, 113, 124, 125, 126, 148, 156, 162, 168, 170.

## Photos by Frank Mecklenburg
Pages 50, 62, 93, 99, 108, 109, 115, 116, 117, 118, 120, 121, 122, 123, 127, 128, 134, 131, 135, 136, 141, 143, 145, 146, 147, 150, 151, 152, 153, 157, 163, 164, 165, 166.

## Permission received from Ezra Ridgley
Historical photos on pages 81, 85.

www.ingramcontent.com/pod-product-compliance
Lightning Source LLC
Chambersburg PA
CBHW070404090426
42733CB00009B/1526